IDEAS
for
THERAPY
with
SEXUAL
ABUSE

Edited by

MICHAEL DURRANT and CHERYL WHITE

Dulwich Centre Publications

© Copyright   1990 by **Dulwich Centre Publications**
ISBN 0 646 01495 1

published by

Dulwich Centre Publications
Hutt St PO Box 7192
Adelaide, Sth Australia 5000
phone (08) 223 3966

Printed and Manufactured in Australia

ACKNOWLEDGEMENTS

We would like to thank Jane Hales for her work in typesetting this book, and for her enduring faith that we would inevitably "run out" of all changes and corrections, and that the final draft would be completed. Her support and encouragement to the authors and editors was invaluable.

Acknowledgement is also due to Alison Turner for graphic designs, and Ray Tyndale for untiring editorial assistance.

C O N T E N T S

INTRODUCTION

Recent years have seen a growing awareness of the prevalence of sexual abuse and its impact on the lives of many of the persons who present to therapists. Having been largely ignored in the therapy literature for many years, sexual abuse is now an issue confronted by therapists who work in a variety of settings. At the same time, attendance at workshops on the topic and comments from therapists suggest that this is an area in which many practitioners feel ill-equipped. Sexual abuse, given such factors as its complexity, the seriousness of its effects, the web of secrecy that often surrounds it, its legal ramifications and the socio-political context within which it occurs, is often viewed as being somehow a 'different' type of problem to those problems encountered in other types of cases. While an appreciation of the particular issues involved in sexual abuse is obviously important for a therapist, regarding it as a problem in a different class has meant that even skilled therapists feel daunted and deskilled. Many persons who embrace ideas from the systems-based family therapy tradition seem to abandon their usual practices and turn to other, more individually and internally focused approaches. Family therapy has been associated with ideas of interaction and with a therapeutic process that is often brief, and these have often been seen as inappropriate for the issue of sexual abuse.

At the same time, it could be argued that its focus on problems occurring within interaction makes family therapy ideally suited to problems of sexual abuse. Many of the systems-based approaches trace their ancestry to the work of Gregory Bateson, and Bateson certainly argued the importance of appreciating the *context* within which interaction occurred. The family therapy field appears, of late, to have stressed family therapy as being a way of conceptualising problems-within-context rather than primarily being a treatment modality defined by the number of persons present. While it is true that insensitive imposition of ideas about always seeing entire families in therapy may have resulted in abusive situations for persons who had been abused, and that 'purist' allegiance to ideas such as circular causality has led family therapists to blur the responsibility of the abuser, there have been a number of therapists applying ideas of interaction-within-context in ways that have been helpful for persons who have experienced sexual abuse.

In particular, therapists in Australia and New Zealand have been at the forefront of innovative thinking about therapy in this context, and ideas from Australian therapists are being applied widely overseas. Two Australian therapists, Kerrie James and Deborah McIntyre, have contributed significantly to the debate about how family therapy should take into account the wider context of violence and abuse, and their work has been cited widely. The work of Michael White, based as it is on ideas about peoples' unique experience of themselves and their problems, and how the particular context of ideas and knowledge influences these experiences, has provided foundation for therapists upon which to build ideas about intervening in situations of violence and abuse.

Within the Australian and New Zealand context, the next logical development was for a book to be published which illustrated the work and thinking of therapists applying these ideas both in Australia and New Zealand, and elsewhere. The book was conceived as a collection of chapters which addressed different, but complementary, aspects of therapy with violence and abuse. Ultimately, this book became two separate volumes. **Invitations to Responsibility: The therapeutic engagement of men who are violent and abusive,** by Alan Jenkins, formed the first part of this project. Alan's book discusses the conceptualisation of the issue of violent and abusive behaviour by men, and proposes a detailed therapy strategy which seeks to invite the men to take responsibility for their behaviour.

This current book forms the second part of the project. The chapters in this volume reflect different emphases and different problem focuses within the area of sexual abuse - adult women, mothers and daughters, families, adolescent abusers, and so on - but share an endeavour to apply ideas from the systemic/cybernetic tradition, an emphasis on persons' unique experiences of their situations and an appreciation of contextual factors. The authors have sought to outline the theoretical and philosophical assumptions which underlie their work and to present practical strategies for therapy with persons for whom sexual abuse has been part of their experience.

We believe that this volume will be useful for anyone who wishes to extend their understanding of, and ideas for, therapy with situations of sexual abuse, whether in working with families, individuals who have experienced abuse, or individuals who have abused. Together with its companion volume, this book provides a detailed resource for therapists in this difficult but important field of work.

Michael Durrant
Eastwood Family Therapy Centre
Epping, New South Wales
Australia

Cheryl White
Dulwich Centre Publications
Adelaide, South Australia
Australia

CHAPTER I

HER-STORY IN THE MAKING:

Therapy with women
who were sexually abused
in childhood

by

Amanda Kamsler

This chapter discusses some of the problematic aspects of the 'traditional' cultural stories about:
- the long term effects on women of child sexual assault, and
- therapy approaches for working with these women when they identify difficulties in their lives.

Some alternative ideas are outlined about how a therapist can participate with women clients who experienced sexual assault in childhood, to enable them to go beyond the oppression of the dominant, pathologizing stories they have about themselves (e.g. stories in which they see themselves as damaged for life), so that they may begin to have access to new, empowering stories about their own resourcefulness and survival. Knowledge gathered from women's stories of their experiences demonstrates how a therapy process that assists clients to locate their experiences in new stories about their resourcefulness leads to them finding and evolving new possibilities for their lives.

Over the last few years I have worked as a therapist in Sydney, Australia, with a number of women who were referred to my practice saying that they were experiencing difficulties which they believed to be related to childhood experiences of sexual assault by male family members or acquaintances. I also work as a consultant for Dympna House, an incest counselling and resource centre for families in which children have been sexually assaulted, and for women who were sexually assaulted in childhood. These experiences have challenged me to re-evaluate my thinking about child sexual assault and to establish clearer ideas about ways of working with the women I see. Ideas outlined in this chapter illustrate some examples from my work and show some applications of these ideas.

For the purposes of this discussion, I propose the following definitions of child sexual assault and incest:

Child sexual assault is a sexual act imposed on a young person or child by another person (usually male). The ability to engage a child in a sexual relationship is based on the all-powerful and dominant position of the adult (or older adolescent) offender, which is in sharp contrast to the child's age, dependency and powerlessness. Authority and power enable the perpetrator to coerce the child into sexual compliance.

Incest is any sexual act imposed on a young person or child by another person (again usually a male), taking advantage of his position of power and trust within the family. 'Family' can mean natural parents, step-parents, grandfathers, uncles, brothers and so on.[1]

Themes in the literature about the long term effects on women of child sexual assault.

A predominant theme in the literature about the effects of child sexual assault is the notion of psychological damage, which the child undergoes as a result of being sexually assaulted and which leaves them with long-term impairments and deficits in their personality. Some writers, such as Ellenson (1985), are interested in identifying these women as having a 'syndrome', describing a set of personality variables commonly manifested by women who were sexually abused as children. These writers propose that the behaviour of women may be assessed using certain criteria from traditional psychiatry. These criteria are used to discuss the 'syndrome', so that doctors and others might diagnose the level of disturbance of the women. Blake-White & Kline (1985) have identified the women's symptoms as fitting with the DSMIII category of post-traumatic stress disorder: *Women who experienced incest as a child have the same pattern of symptoms that identify the syndrome. (p.396)*

They, and other writers in the field, focus on the 'dissociation process', or the 'repression of emotion' which they observe in women who experienced sexual assault in their childhood. Shapiro (1987) holds the view that the woman's ego is 'shattered' and will require 'rebuilding' after such experiences, and this is another common theme in the literature.

Thus the emphasis of many writers has been on the use of traditional psychiatric classification practices to understand and deal with women's responses to child sexual assault. These ideas have had profound implications for the development of ideas about how therapy should be conducted. The goals of therapy have been described in terms like *helping clients get in touch with repressed emotion*; *working through feelings; dealing with repressed memories* (Blake-White & Kline 1985, p.397 & 399); and ... *working through painful experiences and the accompanying guilt and shame, so that conflicts can be revealed, understood, and resolved. (Faria & Belohlavek 1984, p.469)* The act of helping clients to understand the meaning of repressed conflicts is said to produce change. The client comes to terms with her repressed feelings, and this leads to changes in behaviour.

Overall, the terms used to describe approaches to therapy imply that they are based on ideas about diagnosing the client's pathology, which will then be treated by the therapist.

In applying this framework in therapy, the context for the development of the woman's problems is not considered. The attention of therapists has been focussed on ideas like the 'seductive child', or 'pathological mother'. A significant effect of this individual pathology focus is that therapists may overlook the contribution of the perpetrator's interactions with the woman to the development of her perceptions about herself and the world. This effect is understandable in view of the way that the psychiatric literature about incest has largely referred to psychodynamic theory. In the literature, blame has been shifted away from the perpetrators and onto the victims. Waldby (1987) and Ward (1984) provide a clear discussion of the historical origins of this shifting of blame. Elizabeth Ward refers to the clinical literature on incest and finds 'stunning testimony' to what feminist theorists Stanley & Daly have named 'agent deletion'. She describes how the language used in the literature ... *subliminally establishes the wives and daughters as the active parties and the fathers as passive puppets. (p.134)* Her extensive discussion contains graphic examples from the clinical literature which are ... *couched within a cobweb of the same old blame-the-victim mythology. (p.157)*

The literature from family psychiatry offers another set of themes about ways of considering the long term effects on women of child sexual abuse. This body of theory proposes that family dysfunction is the explanation for the existence of incest. The family as a unit is seen as pathological, and symptoms signify overall current family maladjustment. The dysfunctional incestuous family is one in which 'normal' family hierarchies based on age and sex have broken down. This breakdown is attributed almost completely to mothers, who are frequently seen as failing to fulfil their nurturing and protective roles toward the children and their wifely role to the father (Lustig et al 1966; Justice & Justice 1979).

Pathological relationships are viewed as the therapeutic issue, and the occurrence of incest is perceived as a symptom of this. Incest is seen as serving the function of holding together a family system whose internal relationships are unstable.

We propose that incest is a transaction which serves to protect and maintain the family in which it occurs. (Lustig 1966, p.39)

Furniss (1983) supports the idea that incest is a symptom of family dysfunction, saying that:

... the development of the incest dyad between father and daughter is strongly influenced by problems in the mother-daughter and mother-father dyad. (p.267)

His discussion of the father-daughter dyad focusses mainly on the daughter's contribution and his discussion of the mother-daughter dyad focusses mainly on the mother. It is notable that the perpetrator's contribution is only briefly mentioned (Calvert 1984). McCarthy & Byrne (1988) recently made the following statement when commenting on their hypothesis about the link between 'ambivalent social relations' and the generation of incest:

... it seems as if the increased occurrence and disclosure of father-daughter incest is a 'socially situated' phenomenon reflecting the confusion at the heart of the modern family. It is an apparent paradox that this phenomenon is a particular family's somatic expression of its struggle to be child-centred, to shift its gender roles, and to value emotionality, proximity, and non-hierarchical social relations. (p.183)

Once again, the significance of the father's behaviour is obscured in this statement.

Concepts from family therapy such as the view that incest serves a function for the family, or that it may be a family defence against loss (Gutheil & Avery 1977), suggest particular directions for therapy of adult women who experienced child sexual abuse. Therapists operating from these points of view will focus on assisting women to become more 'functional' according to certain criteria for 'normal' family relationships. For example, Deighton & McPeek (1985) describe a family of origin treatment approach in which women in a group are coached to develop a more objective stance with family members and to resolve interpersonal issues with them. They write about the benefit of this being that women begin to see ... *that the adult perpetrator and the non-involved parent were victims too. (p.408)* The authors emphasize the ... *responsibility of the woman in changing her position relative to family of origin members. (p.410)*

These ideas about family dysfunction all obscure the operation of power relationships implicit in incest, and serve to protect the perpetrator and de-emphasize his responsibility. Waldby (1987) says that:

... the daughter's experience is effectively denied by this therapeutic focus,

which regards the actual incestuous relationship as a red herring, whose pursuit may actually impede treatment. (p.15)
In emphasizing the idea that family dynamics should be the focus for therapy, rather than the incest itself (e.g. Machotka 1967), many authors suggest that therapists working with families where incest has occurred assign responsibility to all family members as if they are equally culpable. They see any strong focus on the role of fathers as inappropriate. Thus, therapy based on these notions involves members having to adjust their behaviour to more appropriate roles - particularly, it seems, the traditional roles of mother and daughter.

Thus, while these therapeutic approaches acknowledge the importance of the family context for the development of the woman's problems, they do so in a way which, once again, obscures the power relationship the perpetrator had in his interactions with her in childhood. I believe that these frameworks for therapy promote blindness (or at best, insufficient attention) on the part of the therapist to the responsibility of the perpetrator in shaping the woman's responses and future. As with frameworks which rest on ideas of pathology and diagnosis, the significance of the broader social context is ignored or glossed over in descriptions about these approaches to therapy.

An Alternative View

I agree with Herman (1985) that it is ... *an exaggeration to claim that [child sexual assault and] incest inevitably leads to lasting emotional distress. (p.88)* It is important to note that, as Herman comments, data on long-term effects of father-daughter incest are derived entirely from clinical reports, i.e. studies of women who identified themselves as patients in need of mental health services. She refers to Tsai's (1979) survey which indicated that at least some women with a history of child sexual assault perceive themselves as relatively well-adjusted in adult life, and that this correlated well with clinical assessments. These women acknowledged the trauma of child sexual assault, but believed they had escaped long term distress by receiving helpful intervention from other people, such as family members and teachers.

I hold the view that child sexual assault does not necessarily lead to long-lasting 'intrapsychic damage', e.g. 'shattered ego'. The way I understand what has happened to the women I see in therapy is that they suffer difficulties in their adult life in response to repeating oppressive patterns of interaction in their family and other significant contexts. My perspective is interactional and contextual rather than intrapsychic and psychodynamic.

The more traditional intrapsychic perspectives view the client as having some kind of pathology, which the therapist, as an expert on pathology, will fix through 'diagnosis' and 'treatment'. The implications of this way of thinking is that somehow the damaged personality of the client will be understood and repaired through the expertise of the therapist's interventions. (For further discussion about the implications of various ways of seeing the therapy process, including this way, see Epston & White 1989.)

In contrast to this, a contextual, interactional perspective does not see the development of difficulties as taking place inside the person and as being pervasive to their personality. Instead, attention is paid to the various interactional contexts within which a person's difficulties may emerge.

A contextual way of viewing how difficulties may develop in the life of a woman who was sexually abused in childhood.

• The experience of being sexually abused will initially lead to the young child having an array of confusing and overwhelming feelings, which strongly effect her perception of herself, e.g. she may begin to see herself as bad and dirty and believe she is to blame for the abuse. This is often encouraged by the perpetrator of the abuse, who may work very hard to ensure that the secret about the abuse is kept.

Based on these experiences, and the feelings and beliefs she begins to develop about them, the child begins to develop ways of dealing with her life, e.g. secrecy; blaming herself when things go wrong, which serve to reinforce her feelings and beliefs about herself.

• Following the child's experience of abuse and the establishment of patterns of behaviour and thinking like secrecy and self-blame, the child responds to family members and others in ways which lead them to consider her 'naughty' or 'disturbed', e.g. she may act out sexually, be aggressive or have mood swings. They will respond to her in the ways they usually do when they perceive her as being naughty or disturbed - e.g.

punishment; seek professional help. The perpetrator of the abuse may also be continuing the abuse. All of these interactions serve to reinforce (a) the patterns of behaviour around secrecy and (b) the beliefs the child is developing about herself - e.g. 'I'm no good'. The family context may become a life-support system for these interactions and beliefs, which continue to have a negative affect on her view of herself and on her experience of relationships.

• Disclosure about the abuse may exacerbate the beliefs and behaviour, if the child is not believed. Alternatively, if the child is believed and supported, there may be a significant interruption of the kinds of interactions which secrecy encourages, e.g. more openness may be possible between the child and her mother and siblings. New interactional patterns, challenging secrecy and self-blame, and the breaking of more family silences, become possible.

• If disclosure does not occur, or if the child is not believed and she continues to be influenced by secrecy and self-blame, her experiences as an adult woman of interactions in other significant relationships may further promote the survival of habitual responses and beliefs, e.g. she may blame herself or see herself as damaged if there are sexual problems in her relationship with her partner. She may seek professional help for herself and receive a diagnosis which serves to confirm her view of herself as a damaged person.

Details about the implications of this perspective for therapy will be discussed later in this chapter.

These ideas about the process of the development of difficulties for women who have been sexually assaulted as children are similar to those described by Durrant (1987). He talks about the experience of sexual abuse as one in which the child will have had no control over events when the abuse occurred. This experience of 'out-of-controlness' may be exacerbated by events that follow the abuse, e.g. the disbelief of other people. Durrant describes how the child may become caught up in a cycle of out of control behaviour and emotion, and how the distress may effect all aspects of her experience of herself. This process may continue into adult life.

I believe it is important to include, in this description about the child's family context, an acknowledgement of who it was that had control, i.e. who had the power to define the child's experience and how was this achieved?

I am interested in the notion of including acknowledgement of the responsibility of the perpetrator of the abuse in an account of the development of the woman's difficulties and beliefs about herself. Clearly, there are often other significant relationships which play an important part in shaping a woman's view of herself. I am paying particular attention here to the woman's experience of the relationship with the man who abused her as I believe this has been neglected in the literature.

Oppressive stories authored by perpetrators of child sexual abuse which influence the stories women who were abused tell about themselves.[2]

These ideas are drawn from conversations with women about their experiences in their relationship with the men who sexually abused them.

• It is usually the case that the perpetrator of the abuse has overtly or covertly conveyed to the victim the message that she was to blame for being abused, e.g. 'you led me on'; 'you shouldn't dress like that - you were asking for it'; 'this is all you are good for'. The perpetrator generally denies responsibility for the abuse, for its impact on the child's life and for the consequences to the family. This idea is strongly reinforced for the victim by messages she receives from the surrounding social context, e.g. 'only bad girls get raped'; 'children are seductive'; 'women who get raped must have asked for trouble', and so on. These interactions with the perpetrator will establish the conditions for the development and survival of habits such as self-blame and self-hate. These ways of thinking may permeate the woman's stories about herself.

• The perpetrator will often actively promote secrecy by enforcing it with the child or young woman so that she is divided from other family members. As a child, the woman had no opportunity to check out her own reality because of the rule of secrecy. This contributes to her sense of isolation and confusion, which are devastating side-effects of secrecy. The perpetrator has the power to create a reality for the abuse, perhaps saying things like 'all fathers do this', or 'this is for your own good', or 'you really like this', or 'this is our special secret' to justify his actions. All of this may contribute to the development of self-doubt in the woman's life, as the perpetrator's account of events has had precedence over her own. She may also become vulnerable to erasing her own feelings in response to this.

• The child's interactions with the perpetrator may have encouraged in her feelings of enormous responsibility for others. He may have directly suggested to her things like 'I'll be sent away if you tell', or 'your mother will have a breakdown if you tell her', or 'you're the only one who understands me', or 'I'll go and do this to your little sister if you refuse'. These kinds of ideas might be less directly implied. The effect of this is that the woman has received intensive instruction in putting other's needs first and her own last, and this may become an habitual pattern in her story about relationships.

• The various ways in which the perpetrator exerted control over the child - either subtly or directly, e.g. intimidation, violence - in order to continue to have access to her to meet his needs, may promote the development of habitual responses of fear and panic in intimate relationships when she becomes an adult. Fears may figure prominently in stories she tells about herself (Laing & Kamsler 1988).

Therefore, the woman who was sexually abused in childhood may be seen as not simply under the influence of the past, as Durrant suggests, but also under the influence of a number of prescriptions for how to feel, be and think, which were actively promoted by the perpetrator in his interactions with her.

It is clear that there is a high degree of fit between many of these prescriptions and the predominant role definitions for women which are expressed in patriarchal ideology. Indeed, Waldby (1987) comments:

The kernel of the feminist understanding of incest is formed by the assertion that father-daughter sexual abuse is a particularly intense variant of 'normal' male-female relations in a patriarchal society. (p.17)

She quotes O'Donnell & Craney's idea that the incest victim ... *bears the quintessence of female oppression* - she is introduced to ...*the role of the powerless, dutiful, submissive wife. (as mentioned in Waldby 1987, p.17 & 19)* The child's interactions with the perpetrator can be described as 'intensive training' for her in fitting with the stereotypical submissive female role. The groundwork has been thoroughly prepared for the woman to respond in strongly gendered ways in other significant relationships. She may begin habitually to apply the perpetrator's prescriptions to herself in numerous situations, e.g. putting her own needs aside and developing a 'being for others' lifestyle in her relationships, being passive, being obedient. Thus, the effect of these interactions in childhood may be that she conforms even more strongly to gender prescriptions for women. This perspective about women experiencing the disempowering effects of a relationship which echoes the oppressive arrangements between men and women in society is missing in most of the writings about therapy in the area of child sexual assault.

To sum up, I believe that the significance of the whole context of a woman's experience has been insufficiently explored in the literature which discusses ways of doing therapy with women who were sexually assaulted in childhood. The woman's life is viewed entirely through an intrapsychic lens in the majority of articles about the long term effects of child sexual assault. A consideration of the significance of her experience of interactions with the perpetrator in the development of problems, together with the influence of ideas from the broader social context is entirely left out in many articles and books. This omission frequently leads the therapists to consider the difficulties presented by the woman in therapy as being related to her individual pathology or to dysfunctional family relationships. I believe it is crucial for a therapist to operate from a framework which allows issues from both the woman's familial and social context to be accessed and addressed in therapy.

FRAMEWORK FOR THERAPY

Theory about development of problems.

The framework for therapy that I have started from in working with women is the approach being developed by Michael White, which was initially based on Bateson's cybernetic notions of restraints and information. The pivotal ideas about restraints in cybernetic theory suggest some useful ways to consider the situation of women who were sexually abused as children. The approach understands the development and consolidation of problems in terms of the idea that events take their course because they are restrained from taking alternative courses (White 1986, p.169).

A therapist operating from this perspective constructs the situation of people presenting problems as being a consequence of the operation of retraining beliefs and assumptions about themselves and their world. These beliefs and assumptions do not allow them to have access to alternative solutions to their difficulties. This is because information which does not fit with the restraints is screened out and not perceived. This way of constructing things allows the therapist to view the development of problems as occurring in the context of habitual thoughts and feelings and repeating interactional patterns which prevent the person from having certain information about their own resources which may be useful in solving the problems they are struggling with. For example, a woman who was sexually abused in childhood may habitually blame herself for the abuse, and be unable to 'notice' the perpetrator's contributions to the situation. She can be described as being blind to other information which might assist her in responding differently to the past and present relationships. Clients are seen as being out of contact with information about their own resources which might assist them in handling problems as a result of the operation of restraints. This concept allows us to understand how it is that clients repeatedly apply the same attempted solutions despite the fact that they may in fact perpetuate the problem.

I have already described examples of restraining ideas and patterns in my discussion about the impact of the woman's childhood interactions with the perpetrator, e.g. secrecy.

An example of the way restraints contribute to a woman habitually applying solutions which perpetuate the problem:
A child is sexually abused by her father, who tells her 'All fathers do this - what are you getting upset about?' However, she is upset and anxious and eventually tells a teacher, who does not believe her and tells her not to worry about it. She decides not to tell anyone else. The child believes it is she who has the problem and blames herself for the abuse, and this idea restrains her from making a different response. As an adult whenever she thinks about what happened to her she doesn't tell anyone and continues to think it was her fault. Secrecy and self-blame become strong influences in her life and relationships. Her distress increases - the more this happens, the more she blames herself and it becomes even harder to think about telling someone.

Recently, I have employed White's idea of a text analogy for therapy (White & Epston 1989) which gives another description of the approach. Using this analogy, the development of problems is seen as taking place in the language and conversation of those most concerned about them. People who present to therapists with problems are seen as being intensely focussed on 'problem-saturated' descriptions about their situation and as being out of touch with their capacity to be successful in the face of their difficulties. Problems are seen as a story or idea with a history and a future - being directional, as having a lifestyle support system, and as being progressive, i.e. they are located in a sequence of events across time. People presenting for therapy are said to have co-evolved with others significant to them around certain realities, and the 'dominant story' they tell about themselves (i.e. the problem-saturated description) has been reinforced in many ways, leaving no space for them to perform another story - the story about unique outcomes or occasions where the person was in fact able to have some impact over the problem. Events are interpreted through the lens of this dominant story, which shapes the way persons attribute meaning to their experiences.

An example of how the person's 'dominant story' restrains them from having access to their own resources:
A woman called Alice was referred to me - she was having persistent nightmares, was very concerned that she found it hard to sustain relationsips with men, and saw herself as being irrational and disturbed. She said she had been sexually abused over 6 years by her grandfather when she was a child, and had been physically and emotionally abused by her mother, father and stepmother. She believed that she was a 'mess', and although she thought this was to do with her past experiences, she had accepted family members' views of her as being emotionally disturbed. In her own words 'I'm fucked'. She seemed to have the view that she was a damaged person who was possibly beyond repair. This story pervaded her descriptions of herself so strongly that she was initially unable to identify any information about herself which deviated from the view that she was a 'mess'. She persistently blamed herself for her situation and put herself down - in her own words 'I had a total belief that I was a difficult and unlovable person'. This story was reinforced in her interactions with all family members, who responded to her distress by rejection or withdrawal, and this seemed to lead to her experiencing increased distress which would lead to them seeing her as more disturbed and so on. This story was also perpetuated in her experience of interactions in other significant relationships throughout her life. I will refer to Alice's story in more detail later in this chapter.

In addition to the concepts I have described, I am interested in the idea that the stories people have developed about themselves are located in the context of certain ideologies which are cultural and sociopolitical stories. White has drawn on the work of Foucault in elaborating this idea and suggests that therapy can be a context for challenging the way the ideologies, or dominant knowledges, operate. In relation to incest, I believe the dominant knowledges which influence women in constructing their personal stories are patriarchal ideology and the whole area of psychiatric diagnosis and classification. These are the linguistic and epistemological contexts in which incest has traditionally been located.

Therapy.

What follows from these ideas about problem development is that a context for change can be established through the therapist working to promote double description extensively in therapy. This means that the therapist works with clients to develop many new descriptions of events in order to generate 'news of difference which makes a difference' (White 1986), i.e. to challenge or loosen restraints, including the restraining beliefs from patriarchy and psychiatry. Clients need to be able to draw distinctions, to perceive a contrast between their own description and a new description, for them to receive news of difference or new information. This process triggers new responses which make it possible for them to see new solutions. The new description is co-evolved with the therapist participating actively in introducing new descriptions, often in the form of questions, and building on these new descriptions in response to the clients' responses.

As Munro (1989) says,

Double description challenges restraints, thus triggering new solutions. For example, the second description and the new perceptions this offers, enables clients to experience a view of the problem [and of themselves] which is not bound by the restraints under which their first description operated. (p.185)

The therapist assists the client to develop the new description in a variety of ways which White elaborates in his articles and teaching, e.g. externalizing problems; relative influence questions; collapsing time; raising dilemmas; and responding to responses (White 1986).

These foundation ideas about the approach have been extended in a new direction recently in White's re-description of his work, which he believes fits best with a text analogy for therapy. Clients are seen as being under the influence of a dominant story about themselves, their relationships, and the problem itself. Their descriptions of themselves are understood to be dictated by the dominant story, and the many alternative stories which they could potentially express about their competence and resourcefulness are not given space to be performed. It seems to me that restraints are the beliefs and patterns of interaction that support the dominant story.

The goal of therapy is to invite clients to access aspects of their experience of themselves which have been edited out of the dominant story. The critical steps in assisting clients to locate alternative stories about themselves will be described, together with examples from my work with women who were sexually assaulted in childhood.

Externalizing the problem

Tomm (1989) has described the therapeutic activity of externalizing the problem, which is central to the practice of this approach, as ... *a linguistic separation of the distinction of the problem from the personal identity of the [person].* He believes that this process ... *opens 'conceptual space' for [people] to take more effective initiatives to escape the influence of the problem in their lives. (p.54)* The effect of externalizing the problem is to begin to undo some of the negative effects of diagnosis and labelling. I believe this is of profound importance in the area of child sexual abuse, where, as I have described, there has been a tradition of applying pathologizing, static labels to women. The labelling process encourages conversation in terms of diagnosis. This supports the view that the problem is the woman herself, and reinforces self-blame and guilt. Externalizing the problem is the first step in inviting the woman to separate herself from the effects of labelling, and this leads to the possibility of her noticing alternative stories about herself as a person who at some times has not let the problem entirely overtake her life.

As White (1989) says:

From this new perspective, persons [are] able to locate 'facts' about their lives and relationships that could not even be dimly perceived in the problem-saturated account ... facts that provided the nuclei for the generation of new stories.

The conversations I had in therapy with a woman called Beth contained some examples of externalizing the problem. Beth told me in our early meetings about how she had disclosed to family members that her father had sexually abused her over a number of years when she was a child. She talked extensively about her guilt over the abuse and her fears about coping with life. These feelings had at times in the past pushed her into attempting suicide and believing she was having a 'breakdown'. I externalized secrecy initially, and invited Beth to map its influence on her life and relationships. Fear, guilt and super-responsibility for others appeared to be the major effects and I externalized each of these, e.g. asking her about what impact fear had had in her life, and on her relationships.

Locating the dominant story in the context of interactions, and in the wider social context.

Once the problem has been externalized, the dominant pathologizing story which the woman tells about herself is externalized. I believe it is helpful to assist her to locate where this story came from and to develop some ideas about how it became so influential over time. Questions can be introduced such as: 'How was secrecy encouraged by other people in your life?' 'How was secrecy enforced?' 'What training did you get at favouring others over yourself?' These kinds of questions allow the woman to begin to gain access to the contributions of others, through their interactions with her, to the development of the difficulties she faces. I believe that eliciting a full picture of this is very important, as it facilitates the naming of the oppressive practices which have allowed the effects of child sexual assault to survive. This further assists the woman to separate from the pathologizing picture she has of herself, because she becomes more aware of the whole context of her own experiences, including the context of her interaction with the man who abused her, e.g. when I asked Beth what training she thought she had received in super-responsibility, she talked with me about the ways in which her father had intimidated her so that she would comply with his demands on her (sexual and otherwise); her life as a child became focussed on ensuring that she looked after his needs as a priority.

Questions may potentially be introduced which can assist women to locate their experience of the problem in terms of the limiting effects on them of bigger, socio-political stories or ideologies. For example, I asked

Beth whether she thought that there are ideas in society which might support habits of super-responsibility for women. She readily identified many examples and together we explored the consequences of this for her as a person. White's 1986 paper on anorexia suggests some useful directions for questions which give women an opportunity to assess the impact on them personally of society's prescriptions for women.

Relative Influence Questions.

This approach contains some very helpful ideas about how to invite clients to re-tell their story in such a way that they have access to their experience of their own resourcefulnss in the face of the problem (White 1988, 1989). Two categories of questions can be introduced - one to map out the details and effects of the dominant story, e.g. What influence have fears had on your life? on your relationships with other people?, and one to begin to map out the 'unique outcomes', or the occasions where the woman experienced some influence in her own life despite the power of the dominant story. For example, any disclosure of sexual abuse is a direct attack on secrecy, and is a unique outcome. A woman may be asked whether she had ever told anyone she was sexually abused, and this could be followed by an exploration, e.g 'How was it that you defied the secrecy when you disclosed about your father abusing you?' It is crucial that a thorough exploration of the first category of questions, about the dominant story, is entered into before unique outcomes questions are introduced.

It is not my intention to cover the many and varied ways a client can be invited to identify unique outcomes. However, when the therapist asks unique outcome questions like: 'Was there an occasion when you could have been stopped in your tracks by fear but you withstood it instead?', space is opened for the client to begin to author an alternative story about herself.

Questions to invite an elaboration of the alternative story.

The client is invited to 'perform meaning' around the unique outcomes which are identified. The kinds of questions asked ensure that the woman is able to attribute personal meanings to events and to experience the impact of the new emerging story. This is a prerequisite for the survival of the new story. The client is invited to locate a full account of the unique outcomes in a new, alternative story about her lived experience. The goal of this is to ensure that the person experiences the full significance of the unique outcomes. This process of inviting people to go back to their own experience and bring forth alternative stories about themselves leads to them having a different experience of themselves. The role of the therapist throughout therapy could best be described as co-author of these emerging alternative stories.

The following questions came from my conversations with Beth: How was it that you defied secrecy and your father's training in putting others first, when you disclosed about the abuse?

When Beth identified some other occasions when she had put herself first, I enquired about them in detail:

- *How were you able to do this?*
- *How did you give yourself priority?*
- *How do you account for the fact that you felt strong enough to withstand the habit of putting others first?*
- *How did you withstand your father's training?*
- *What did you experience?*
- *What difference has this made to your experience of yourself?*
- *What does this tell you about yourself that you didn't realize before?*
- *How could you bring your friends up to date with this development?*

There are countless ways a therapist can participate with the client to develop and extend the alternative story. White's articles outline the kinds of questions which appear most likely to further the co-authoring of alternative stories.

The application in therapy of ideas such as externalizing problems and unqiue outcome questions allows the therapist to assist the woman to locate her experience in the context of family interactions, including the relationship with the perpetrator. It also allows her to locate her experience in terms of the broader socio-political context. In the process of therapy, the woman has the opportunity, in conversation with the therapist, to discover information about herself and her resources. This leads to her responding in ways which pave the way for change. The emphasis here is on the idea of the client as expert, with the therapist's role being to ask questions which generate unique outcomes and new stories. This is in contrast to more traditional ways of doing therapy, where the therapist is seen as the expert who has the knowledge to diagnose and fix the client's problems.

The approach outlined here taps knowledges a woman has about herself and her strengths, which have been buried as a result of the operation of the dominant story. When the woman is invited to separate herself from the dominant story, and new information is generated, the dominant knowledges which the woman draws upon to define herself are thereby challenged, and new responses and solutions become available to her.

THE STORY OF ALICE: An illustration of the therapy process.

Alice is a woman I have seen in therapy over the last 2 years. She has agreed to allow me to share this story, which includes her comments on her experience as a client which she decided to write down as a way of reviewing it for herself.[3]

Alice was referred to me by a therapist at Dympna House, where she had participated in a self-help group for incest survivors. When she contacted me to make an appointment, she said she wanted help in two areas:

• Handling her nightmares. Over the last 2 years she had been experiencing long periods of disturbed sleep as a result of terrifying dreams. The nightmares would persist over months, occasionally disappear for short periods, then suddenly recur for months on end.

• When she was involved in relationships with men, she would feel comfortable for a short time, but end up feeling revulsed in sexual situations. She would often finish relationships based on this. She saw this as being related to her experiences of sexual abuse.

Alice said that she had sought therapy earlier in her life to deal with her distress about her family and with her memories about being sexually abused by her grandfather. Individual and group therapy had helped to some degree, and she said that she had felt that she was not so alone on learning that the experience of child sexual abuse was a common one among women. However, despite her previous attempts to get help, she was still feeling very distressed and confused about her life.

Alice began by presenting to me her concerns about her nightmares and relationships. She also talked about her experiences of being sexually abused by her grandfather from age 4 to age 11. Her parents had separated in the UK when she was 3 years old, and her father was given custody of her as her mother was seen as being 'emotionally unstable'. She and her father came to Australia where her father met and married his second wife. It was this woman's father who sexually abused her. She described how she had disclosed about the sexual abuse to her stepmother during adolescence, but was not believed until her stepsister disclosed that the same thing was happening to her. No action was ever taken outside the family over this - the stepmother confronted her father, but did not support Alice. Alice described the ongoing conflict which she had with her stepmother and father, which led to her being asked to leave home at 17. In Alice's view, every interaction with members of her family - including the infrequent contact with her mother - was an experience of rejection and invalidation.

The focus of the first three sessions was not on nightmares, sexual abuse or current relationships with men. Alice talked with me in detail about her worry about therapy and her distrust of therapists. I took the sessions slowly, believing that her worry about trusting me was an important restraint in the relationship with me. I asked her to simply consider the risks of getting involved in therapy and to begin to keep track of the occurrence of the nightmares in a diary.

Alice noticed during the first three sessions that she was experiencing more sadness, and began to talk about how difficult and uncomfortable it was for her to show her feelings to other people. This she saw as a big risk in being involved in therapy, where she might get more in touch with herself and her needs and feelings. She voiced her fear that 'there is so much there' that she wasn't sure that she or the therapist would cope. I externalized her habit of hiding feelings, and we explored the effect of this on her life. I discovered that she had received training from family members in not showing feelings as this meant she was 'irrational' and 'bad' like her mother was. Her mother was portrayed to her as incompetent and volatile. She said that she had learnt by her experiences of rejection and the disbelief of other family members when she was upset that no one could handle her feelings, so she just coped on her own with them. We talked about how she had learnt not to be herself, developing the habit of being someone else's kind of person rather than being her own person (another externalization) in response to family members' requests to not be so emotional. She talked about her isolation, and cried about how sad she felt that no one in her family had supported her or believed her distress about the sexual abuse.

I began to attempt to get a picture of the unique outcomes by asking Alice whether there had ever been occasions where she had rebelled against these habits and prescriptions and been herself in relationships. She identified occasions where she had taken risks and asked for support from friends. I asked her to supply some details about how she had been able to do this, given the intensive training she had had in not being herself and hiding herself. I also talked with her about how it was she was able to challenge the training, in allowing herself to feel so much during our meetings.

During the first three sessions, Alice's nightmares disappeared - the more she acknowledged her sadness and fear, the less she experienced it at night. She also took the step of contacting the state welfare department and giving them information about her grandfather, although she did not lay charges. I responded to this information with questions to extend the account about unique outcomes, e.g. how had she had the courage to be herself in these situations? It was in session 3 that Alice first talked with me about her habits of peeling skin off her face and arms, and of bingeing and vomiting. She had never told anyone about these habits before. I externalized them, using the word 'habits' to describe them. I believe this was another breakthrough in Alice challenging the effects of her training in not being herself. Alice said quite strongly that she did not wish to focus on these habit as they were not really that much of a problem at present. This continued until later in therapy.

Sessions 4 - 6

Alice continued to report having nightmare-free nights and to make changes in being more open about her vulnerability to friends and some family members. She made further disclosures to me about being violently physically abused by both her mother and stepmother and we talked about how this had fed her developing habit of not being herself, of self-invalidation and self-depreciation (further externalizations). It became clear to me from her descriptions about feeling ripped off by others in her family that the sexual abuse was only one way in which Alice had experienced invalidation of herself as a person.

An important focus of this part of the therapy was on seizing on any information Alice gave me about unique outcomes, e.g. times she was open to other people about her feelings. I would elicit the details around these events to allow for a performance of meaning about her escape from her habits of self-invalidation. I was also able to develop with Alice an account of her survival strategies when she was growing up, so that I might understand how she had stopped herself from being completely overtaken by self-invalidation. She recounted her story of survival as a child by describing how she wrote stories and poetry which expressed her feelings. This was a special and precious thing she did when she locked herself in her room, to have breathing space from family conflicts. I asked her whether there were any survival strategies which she had continued to use in the present, and she identified that she was still valuing her own self-expression through singing and occasionally through writing songs. She was able to tell me that she was removing herself from some situations where she was feeling 'done over'. I described this as trusting herself, and as going against her habit of self-invalidation. Once again, I explored the details of these occasions of self-validation to encourage a performance of meaning around them.

Alice made further small but significant changes in the direction of valuing herself and being more true to herself. However, she frequently trivialized her achievements. She said she kept seeing herself as 'fucked', and this made it hard for her to notice changes. When I talked with her about whether she thought she was ready to take any further steps in the new direction, she began to talk about her fears in relation to having to start a new life as a different sort of person if she went further with the changes. At this point, I restrained further changes. I invited her to keep track of any examples of occasions where she was being true to herself or valuing herself.

Sessions 7 - 10

When I enquired about the extent to which self-appreciation was evident in her life, versus the extent of self-depreciation, Alice began to describe more examples of times when she had valued something about herself. I gathered a lot of details about these examples, and she then spontaneously recalled further occasions of self-appreciation. As this progressed, Alice noticed that she had started to break with her habit of being for others in friendships and of putting others' needs before her own. *The most important strategy for me was to acknowledge and leave behind contexts that continued to arouse and create pain.*

Once I was able to do this I was able to construct new ways of interacting with people, in more positive and self-gratifying relationships. I didn't insist on maintaining relationships out of guilt or self-destruction, and saw the benefits of trusting people and establishing supportive relationships. (Alice 1988)

At this point, she once again started to talk about her habit of bingeing and vomiting, saying that it was happening more often. I got some details about this by asking her about the effect bulimia had had on her life, and she was able to talk with me about some periods of her life where she had escaped bulimia, as well as about how she had achieved this (tracking unique outcomes). During this phase of therapy, Alice put me in the picture about further ways she had been in training to see herself as 'fucked' (e.g. significant upsetting interactions with her mother), and the ways in which she thought she had been effected by this training, e.g. hiding herself, fears of rejection if she was more herself, and seeing herself as being responsible for everything that has gone wrong in her life. I talked with her about the habit of bulimia being a way she could be less 'herself', and this was an idea she could connect with. I suggested she keep track of times where she refused bulimia's invitations (tracking unique outcomes).

Sessions 11 - 14

Alice began to have some victories over bulimia, and for the first time to allocate more responsibility to family members for her distress. I explored these developments in detail describing them as achievements in self-appreciation. I talked with her about her ideas about how bulimia had originally become so influential in her life. She identified the origin of many secret habits in her life, including bulimia, in response to the extreme reactions of her parents to her developing sexuality. I also asked her about things like in what ways she thought she had subjected herself to fitting with ideal images for women in terms of shape. I enquired about whether she thought these images might further have encouraged her to be less than herself, and she agreed this may have been the case. We talked in detail about the occasions where she had beaten bulimia, and as sessions went on she had more victories over it. In response to this, I asked her questions like: How do you think it was possible for you to allow yourself to be more fully yourself on that occasion? How were you able to break away from subjecting yourself to society's prescriptions for thinness for women, and to appreciate yourself in this way?

In some of my questions I was inviting her to identify the influence on her personally of the broader social context of patriarchy which supports the idea of women being less than themselves, or invalidating themselves. I was also inviting her to consider ways she had been for herself and had withstood these prescriptions.

Alice experienced a period of anxiety in response to the changes she was making. She talked about being worried about losing her 'old self' - who would she become? She also described her habit of picking at herself for the first time in more detail. We tracked the story about how this habit had become stronger recently. I was also able to locate some unique outcomes, or occasions where she had not given in to the habit. However, Alice said she was unsure about whether she wanted to talk further about this habit. I asked her to consider the consequences of talking further about it in therapy.

Alice then began to recall some frightening situations which happened to her as a child at bedtime, and together we recognized how the picking habit had become an ally to fear. It had become away to hypnotize herself and stop fear, and another way to 'lose herself'. I suggested that she schedule half an hour each night for this habit so that she might get more information about how it helped her with her fears. To use Alice's own words:

Upfront acknowledgement, and giving myself permission to include these [habits] in moderation, allowed me to change my perspective on these behaviours and slowly take control of them.

Alice was noticing at this stage that she was no longer letting her distress in any one area of her life overwhelm all the others, and that she experienced a sense of feeling more in control.

It was clear that Alice was experiencing more control over her self-destructive habits. She recognized readily how she was able to stop herself from being taken over by them - our conversation contained more spontaneous examples from her about this, and less examples about being overwhelmed by the habits. She discovered many new strategies for handling her fears at night, e.g. by listening to music to help her relax.

The problem-saturated description was taking up less space in therapy and Alice was constructing a new story for herself. When I explored how all this had been achieved, Alice said:

I've changed my ideology about myself. At first I thought, 'I'm fucked.' Then I moved on to thinking, 'They're fucked', about my family. Now I believe that I'm OK - I have my problems in life, but I am OK and I am healing myself.

She also said that she felt less anxious and worried about herself generally, and this meant that she had more space to deal with the self-destructive habits.

To encourage a performance of meaning around these numerous changes, I asked her about what difference this new view of herself was making to the way she treated herself day to day; what difference this made to her relationships with family and with friends; and about what new possibilities these changes might open up for her.

I predicted 'hiccups' with the habits and we discussed how she might deal with them, e.g. scheduling in time for the picking habit.

Alice has maintained the changes, with bulimia and picking at herself almost disappearing from her life. She has formed new relationships in which she experiences caring and acknowledgement. She says she now believes she is competent and is actively achieving changes in her own life. She describes the experience of seeing herself in a context when problems occur, i.e. she no longer labels herself as a problem when things go wrong. She reports feeling good and valuing herself in the presence of people who have been problematic for her in the past. She has had some hiccups, but does not feel overwhelmed when they occur. She has made many steps, which she has drawn my attention to, in being more fully herself, in valuing herself, and in being less a person for others and more for herself.

I have stopped having regular sessions with Alice and have invited her to contact me if she wants to review things with me. I recently saw her when she experienced a hiccup in relation to the breakup of a relationship. She continues to experience a sense of control over her own life, e.g. recently she has come up with the idea of using her dreams as resources to herself.

I'm not perfect, I'm still self-critical and constantly striving for self-improvement - but I'm OK and I like myself and despite my normal emotional ups and downs, I understand myself and my reactions and I now feel in control and able to move on past the pain of my past. (Alice, August 1988)

CONCLUSION

In conclusion, I believe that there are many unhelpful, limiting and potentially oppressive ideas being applied in the service of therapy with women who were sexually abused as children. My preference has been for a framework which acknowledges and accesses the influence of familial and relationship contexts (including the context of the woman's relationship with the man who abused her), as well as the influence of restraining ideas from patriarchal ideology, in the process of the development of problems in the woman's life. Therapy may be seen as an opportunity to address restraints or dominant stories, through the therapist assisting the woman to generate double descriptions or alternative stories; this allows the woman a chance to re-tell her story about herself. It has been my experience, in approaching therapy like this, that many women have responded by strongly challenging the dominant stories in creative ways, finding solutions which have been empowering for them.

NOTES

1.   These are the definitions adopted by Dympna House.
2.   I wish to acknowledge the original work of Lesley Laing, who was the instigator for ideas expressed in this section of the chapter.
3.   I would like to acknowledge the valuable contribution of Catherine Munro, with whom I consulted at various stages of this process.

ACKNOWLEDGEMENTS

I wish to thank Lesley Laing and Catherine Munro, who have each made particular and special contributions in helping me develop ideas which have been critical to the writing of this chapter. I am very grateful to both of them for their assistance with various drafts of the chapter, and for their invaluable support. I am grateful to Bronwyn Cintio for her assistance in the early stages of writing the chapter. Finally, I wish to thank Michael White for his encouraging comments about the chapter, Steven Kamsler and Melanie Kamsler for their loving support.

REFERENCES

Blake-White, J. & Kline, C.M. 1985:
'Treating the dissociative process in adult victims of childhood incest.' **Social Casework**, September, p.394-402.
Calvert, G. 1984:
'Letter to the Editor.' **Australian Journal of Family Therapy**, 5:1.
Deighton, J. & McPeek, P. 1985:
'Group treatment: adult victims of child sexual abuse.' **Social Casework**, September, p.403-410.
Durrant, M. 1987:
'Therapy with young people who have been the victims of sexual assault.' **Family Therapy Case Studies**, 2(1):57-63.
Ellenson, G. 1985:
'Detecting a history of incest: a predictive syndrome.' **Social Casework**, November, p.525-532.
Faria, G. & Belohlavek, N. 1984:
'Treating female adult survivors of childhood incest.' **Social Casework**, October, p.465-471.
Furniss, T. 1983:
'Family process in the treatment of intra-familial child sexual abuse.' **Journal of Family Therapy**, 5:263-278.
Gutheil, T. & Avery, N. 1977:
'Multiple overt incest as family defence against loss.' **Family Process**, p.105-116.
Herman, J. 1985:
'Father-daughter incest.' In Burgess, A. (Ed.) **Rape & Sexual Assault – a research handbook**.
Justice, B. & Justice R. 1979:
The Broken Taboo: Sex in the family. Human Sciences Press, New York.
Laing, L. & Kamsler A. 1988:
Training workshops for therapists working with women who were sexually abused in childhood. Sydney.
Lustig, N. et al. 1966:
'Incest: a family group survival pattern.' **Archives of General Psychiatry**, 14:31-40.
Machotka, P. et al. 1967:
'Incest as a family affair.' **Family Process**, 6:98-116.
McCarthy, I.D. & Byrne, N.O. 1988:
'Mis-taken love: conversations on the problem of incest in an Irish context.' **Family Process**, 27(2):181-199.
Munro, C. 1989:
'White and the cybernetic therapies: news of difference.' **Australian & New Zealand Journal of Family Therapy**, 8(4):183-192.

O'Donnell, C. & Craney, J. 1982:
'Incest and the reproduction of the patriarchal family.' In O'Donnell, C. & Craney, J. (Eds.) **Family Violence In Australia**. Longman, Cheshire.

Shapiro, S. 1987:
'Self-mutilation & self-blame in incest victims.' **American Journal of Psychotherapy**, 41(1):46-54.

Tomm, K. 1989:
'Externalizing the problem and internalizing personal agency.' **Journal of Strategic & Systemic Therapies**, 8:1.

Tsai, M. et al. 1979:
'Childhood molestations: psychological functioning in adult women.' **Journal of Abnormal Psychology**, 88:407-417.

Waldby, C. 1987:
'Theoretical Perspectives on Incest: A Survey of the Literature in Breaking the Silence: A report based upon the findings of the Women Against Incest Phone-In Survey (Sydney, 1984).' Researched and written by Cathy Waldby. Dympna House.

Ward, E. 1984:
Father Daughter Rape. The Women's Press, London.

White, M. 1986:
'Negative explanation, restraint & double description: a template for family therapy.' **Family Process**, 25:2:169-184.

White, M. 1986:
'Anorexia Nervosa: a cybernetic perspective.' In Elka-Harkaway, J. (Ed.) **Eating Disorders**. Aspen Publishers, Maryland,

White, M. 1988:
'The process of questioning: a therapy of literary merit?' **Dulwich Centre Newsletter**, Winter.

White, M. 1988-89:
'The externalizing of the problem.' **Dulwich Centre Newsletter**, Summer.

White, M. & Epston, D. 1989:
Literate Means to Therapeutic Ends. Dulwich Centre Publications, Adelaide.

C H A P T E R   II

USING RITUALS

to
Empower Family Members
Who Have Experienced
Child Sexual Abuse

by

Janet Adams-Westcott
&
Deanna Isenbart

In all families, rituals are an important part of development across the life cycle. In families who have experienced intrafamily child sexual abuse, development is arrested and ritual behaviour is underdeveloped, rigid, or hollow. This chapter examines the multiple uses of the ritual process, normative rituals, and therapeutic rituals with members of families who have experienced incest. The ritual process is described within the context of a cybernetic model of intrafamily child sexual abuse. This model is informed by the theory and therapy of Michael White.

Rituals are described that:

• help family members free themselves of those beliefs and patterns of interaction that contribute to child sexual abuse;

• facilitate the development of individuality and a sense of personhood;

• help family members redescribe themselves and their experiences in a less restrained and more resourceful manner; and

• empower family members to recognize and solidify the changes that occur as a result of the therapeutic process.

THERAPY AND THE RITUAL PROCESS

Rites of passage

In his study of developmental transitions across the life cycle, anthropologist van Gennep (cited in Roberts 1988) described how rites of passage assist people in moving from one status to another. Rites of passage begin when persons separate from an old status that no longer fits for them. They then experience a period characterized by disorganization and experimentation with new ideas and behaviours. When the transition is successfully negotiated, the ideas and behaviours are incorporated into the person's description of self. At this point, the community recognizes that change has occurred and awards the person a new status.

Koback & Waters (1984) applied this three phase process to family therapy. Therapy is conceptualized as a ritual that facilitates the transition of family members from an old status that was seen as problematic or symptomatic to a new status that focuses on resources and includes opportunities for growth.

Therapeutic rituals

The use of rituals as a therapeutic technique was first described by the Milan team (Selvini Palazzoli et al 1977, 1978). These therapists prescribed rituals to create clarity in situations where family members experienced confusion due to contradictory beliefs or rules (Tomm 1984). Rituals developed by the Milan team included specific tasks that were offered to families as potentially useful experiments. The particular task was chosen to help family members resolve contradictions and discover alternative patterns of interaction.

The odd days and even days task is among the many rituals described by the Milan team (Selvini Palazzoli et al 1978). The ritual was originally developed for a family where the parents were concerned about a disruptive child. The team hypothesized that differences in the styles of discipline used by the parents were contributing to the problematic behaviours. They suggested that one parent assume responsibility for discipline on odd days. On even days, the other parent was responsible for discipline. On those days when they were not in charge of discipline, each parent was instructed to observe the interaction between the child and their partner. The ritual created clarity for the child who knew what style of parenting to expect on a particular day. The ritual also provided the parents the opportunity to discover the benefits of consistency and working together.

The use of rituals as a therapeutic technique has been further elaborated by Evan Imber-Black (1988) and her colleagues (Imber-Black, Roberts & Whiting 1988). These authors have identified five themes which assist therapists in the design and implementation of rituals:

Membership. Therapeutic rituals can be used to define family membership and facilitate entrances into and exits from family systems. Membership rituals can be designed to create boundaries, both inside the family and in relationship to the outside world.

Healing. When family members have experienced the loss of significant persons, relationships, health, roles, or hopes for the future, rituals can be developed to promote healing. Healing rituals can also be designed to facilitate the process of forgiveness and reconciliation.

Identity Definition and Redefinition. Rituals can be developed to help people escape the effects of an identity as a problematic person. When people have adopted unrealistic descriptions of themselves that don't fit for them, rituals can be designed to help them redefine their expectations and change their relationship with themselves.

Belief Expression and Negotiation. When family members hold conflicting ideas about an issue, rituals can be used to create a context for the appreciation of difference. A new pattern of interaction is established when family members can experience each other's perspectives without blame.

Celebration. Therapeutic rituals can be developed to punctuate change, mark accomplishments, and facilitate life cycle transitions. These celebrations are often incorporated into the family's ongoing traditions. Therapists can work with family members to co-create celebrations that serve to inform significant persons about changes.

THE THEORY AND THERAPY
OF MICHAEL WHITE

Narrative Epistemology: The dominant story

The use of rituals to empower persons who have experienced intrafamily child sexual abuse is situated within the model for therapy developed by Michael White (1986a, 1986b, 1986c, 1986d, 1986e, 1988a, 1988b, 1989; White & Epston 1989). The model assumes that, in order to make sense out of lived experiences, persons organize these experiences into a dominant story about themselves and their relationships. Dominant stories create a 'perceptual lens' that influences the meaning that persons ascribe to subsequent life events. Information that is consistent with the dominant story is selected out and expressed in behaviour. People tend not to notice or give meaning to those aspects of lived experience that do not 'fit' the dominant narrative. The dominant stories that people develop about themselves and their relationships may be empowering and generative or disempowering and oppressive.

Problem formation

Problems develop when dominant stories include restraints which prevent people from noticing new information that might lead to more useful solutions. White (1986a, 1986d) considers two kinds of restraints:

- The system of beliefs that make up the dominant story of family members can create restraints that contribute to the development and maintenance of problems. White (1986a, 1987, 1989) is particularly interested in normative expectations about how people should be as individuals and in relationships. White argues that these specifications of personhood and relationships are often experienced as oppressive, given that people inevitably fail to measure up to such standards.
- People are also restrained by vicious cycles. Vicious cycles include those habitual patterns of interaction that maintain problematic behaviours. Family members are generally unaware that their interaction is patterned and perceive themselves as having no choice but to continue to participate in the vicious cycle.

Problem Resolution

Externalizing the problem

White's therapy techniques assist family members in challenging those restraining beliefs and patterns of behaviour that contribute to disempowering dominant stories. The technique of externalizing the problem is used to separate the person from the problem and/or restraints that maintain the dominant story. The problem is located outside of the person or relationship that has been identified as having the problem. It is objectified and given a name (White 1989).

The process of separating the problem from the person promotes personal agency (Tomm 1989; White 1989). Family members become aware that they can choose to continue to participate in vicious cycles that maintain the problem or they can choose to interact in nonproblematic ways.

Developing an alternative story

Questions are asked which help family members locate aspects of their lived experience that are not consistent with the dominant story (White 1988a, 1989). These experiences are then connected via questions that examine past and present exceptions to the dominant story, as well as intentions to resist the problem in the future. Questions are then asked that encourage family members to redescribe themselves in a more empowering manner and to develop alternative stories about themselves, their relationships, and their future. The alternative story is maintained through techniques that circulate this new descripton to significant others in their lives.

The Ritual Process

The rites of passage analogy has been used to conceptualize change within the context of White's model (White 1985, 1986e; White & Epston 1989). The model assumes that people present for therapy when significant aspects of their lived experience contradict the dominant narrative about themselves and their relationships. The process of externalization helps people separate from the archaic aspects of their dominant stories. Questions are asked that invite people to experiment with new ideas and behaviours. Persons achieve a new status when they incorporate these changes into an alternative story that is more consistent with the full range of their lived experience. The rites of passage analogy assumes that symptoms and crises are evidence of 'progress rather than regress' (White & Epston 1989, p.17).

White and his colleagues have described a number of rituals they have co-created with family members to challenge problem-saturated dominant stories (c.f. Durrant 1989; Epston 1989; White 1986c, 1986e). A ritual developed to help children escape fears provides one example: the process of externalization begins by examining the influence of fear on the child and family members. Next, family members are invited to consider those times when they have been able to minimize or escape fear. The child is encouraged to personify the fear by drawing it and giving it a name. The picture of the fear or monster is then secured in a box and the child is invited to engage in a variety of 'fear busting and monster taming' activities. These tasks emphasize the child's competence in relationship to fear. The parents historicize the child's accomplishments by taking pictures of the various activities. The therapist awards the child with a trophy or certificate declaring expertise in fear busting and monster taming.

RESTRAINTS CREATING VULNERABILITY
TO CHILD SEXUAL ABUSE

Traditional conceptualizations of intrafamily child sexual abuse describe families who experienced incest as the most 'dysfunctional' and the most 'resistant' to change. Intervention focuses on resolving the trauma of the victim, confronting the psychopathology of the offender, and changing dysfunctional family dynamics (c.f. Alexander 1985; Trepper & Barrett 1986, 1989).

A cybernetic conceptualization of child sexual abuse views family members who have experienced abuse as 'restrained' by disempowering dominant stories. Restraining beliefs and patterns of behaviour prevent access to resources and impede the changes that are necessary for growth and development across the life cycle. Intervention serves as a rite of passage to help family members:

- escape disempowering dominant stories,
- challenge restraints that create vulnerability to abuse, and
- utilize strengths to develop alternative and more empowering stories.[1]

Restraining beliefs

Intrafamily abuse is associated with rigid and unrealistic specifications of personhood and family relationships. Patriarchal ideology and rigid adherence to traditional roles of men and women are among the societal factors that have been identified as perpetuating family violence (Straus, Gelles & Steinmetz 1980; White 1986a, 1986b). These beliefs legitimize violence by placing men in a position of supremacy over women and children, who are perceived as property. The negative consequences of patriarchal ideology are illustrated by empirical studies which indicate that 90% of perpetrators of sexual assault are men or boys (Finklehor 1986).

Vulnerability to victimization is increased when the dominant cultural story about what is expected of women contributes to beliefs and expectations that compromise the growth of the individual. This occurs when girls and women are restrained from developing a sense of personhood apart from their roles as daughters, mothers, or wives. They expect to nurture and take care of others, but do not expect to be taken care of in return (Gelinas 1986).

Beliefs about family loyalty that place priority on maintaining the integrity of the family at the expense of individual members provide a second source of risk for victimization. These beliefs often extend across generations. Family rules such as 'You don't care about me if you disagree with me' impede the development of a sense of personhood that is necessary for children to grow up and leave home (Alexander 1985; Gelinas 1986; Barrett, Sykes & Barnes 1986).

Children who experience these restraining specifications are likely to develop a picture of themselves as having few resources. They measure their self-worth on the extent to which they are self-denying and are a 'person for others' rather than 'a person from themselves'. They may develop a 'victim lifestyle' characterized by feelings of powerlessness and passive behaviour.

The beliefs that persons who have experienced abuse develop about themselves restrain them from noticing their strengths. They are blind to those aspects of their lived experience that contradict their view of themselves as helpless, powerless, and incompetent. They fail to select out or ascribe meaning to times when they behaved in a competent manner or to experiences where others treated them as a person of worth (Durrant 1987; Kowalski & Durrant 1989).

Negative beliefs about self and traditional beliefs about the male role create restraints on behaviour that contribute to vulnerability to perpetrating sexual abuse. Boys and men are restrained from developing richness of emotional expression. Traditional male stereotypes allow the expression of anger, while limiting expressions of emotions such as sadness, grief, or fear. Restricted emotional expression interferes with one's ability to understand the perspective of the other and experience empathy (Gondalf 1985). A father whose map of the world does not allow him to understand the devastating consequences of sexual abuse for his children is at high risk of engaging in abusive behaviour (Jenkins 1987).

For many sexual abusers, their own childhood history of emotional, physical, or sexual abuse contributes to negative beliefs about self. A vicious cycle is set up when low self-esteem interferes with the development of social skills in childhood and adolescence and thus the development of rewarding peer relationships as an adult. This negative map is maintained by the discrepancy between idealized views of men as strong and competent and the perpetrator's own experience of self as insecure and inadequate.

Unable to experience competency in adult relationships, these men may turn to children to obtain emotional nurturing and sexual gratification (Finklehor 1986). Within the context of their dominant story, this exploitation may be interpreted as evidence of power and mastery.

Interactional Restraints

Patterns of interaction which restrain change increase vulnerability to the development of intrafamily child sexual abuse. Risk for incest is highest in families where members interact in patterns that insulate them from new ideas that might challenge their dominant story. Isolation is one mechanism through which change is avoided. Opportunities for interaction and emotional closeness are restricted to other family members (Alexander 1985).

Interactions which discourage individual preferences and differences of opinion provide a second mechanism through which change is restrained. In extreme cases, there is little separation between the feelings and thoughts expressed by family members. They appear to have a joint identity based on their system of shared beliefs. Privacy and personal belongings may be given little value. Any move by one family member in the direction of individual growth is met by invitations from other family members to return to the old ways of interaction (Alexander 1985).

Patterns of interaction that maintain high levels of denial contribute to the development and maintenance of abusive behaviour. Through complementary patterns of interaction, family members invite each other to ignore or distort information that would suggest particular behaviours are inappropriate or hurtful. It is through the process of denial that sexually abusive behaviour develops and is maintained. Family members may deny:

- the existence of abuse,
- awareness of particular events,
- responsibility for the abuse, and
- the impact of abuse on the victim (Barrett et al 1986; Sykes & Winn 1989; Jenkins 1987).

In retrospective reports, non-offending mothers can often identify clues that might have led them to suspect sexual abuse. Invitations to deny the significance of the behaviour interfered with their ability to interpret their spouse's behaviour as inappropriate at the time it was occurring.

THE RITUAL PROCESS AND INTERVENTION
IN CHILD SEXUAL ABUSE
Separation Phase

In families who have experienced incest, disclosure marks the beginning of a separation from a very closed, isolated, and secretive lifestyle. Frequently, there is emotional separation within the family, whereby each family member views himself or herself as pressured to align his or her loyalties with either the offender or with the victim. Physical separation of family members may occur when either the offender or the victim is removed from the home.

The secretive lifestyle family members have led is replaced by a lifestyle of observation by social control agents. Family members often experience helpers as 'intruders' who victimize them through labels as 'sick' or 'bad'. The involvement of the larger system may be experienced by some family members as controlling their lives or robbing them of choices. Many parents react with anger and resist co-operating with suggestions or demands made by the larger system.

Membership: Introducing a new story

In initial contacts with family members, especially those who are court referred, it is important to separate the experience of 'psychotherapy' from this oppressive view of the helping system. The intake process can be structured to serve as a therapeutic ritual to introduce family members to a new description of 'outside helpers'. This process also empowers family members to begin to develop new descriptions of themselves as persons with choices. They are encouraged to actively participate in plotting the direction of their therapeutic experience. Treatment goals are co-created by individual family members and the therapy team.

Belief Negotiation: Challenging restraints

The intake process can also be designed to begin the process of externalizing those restraining beliefs and interactions that contribute to vulnerability to abuse. Family members are offered a description by the therapist that suggests that intrafamily child sexual abuse occurs only in families which are vulnerable. The therapist assists parents in identifying the kinds of ideas or interactions that contributed to the development and maintenance of sexual abuse in their family. The therapist helps the parents identify examples of how they have been pushed around by these beliefs and vicious cycles for a long time before the sexual abuse occurred. With the onset of abuse, family members get more under the influence of these factors and less and less in control of their own lives. The goal of therapy is then identified as helping family members take charge of their lives and escape those factors that created vulnerability to sexual abuse.

By separating persons from problematic beliefs or interactions, parents become aware of their participation in the problem. They begin to develop a sense of personal agency. They can choose to side with the problematic ways of thinking and behaving, or side against them.

This description is introduced in the context of a six-week psycho-educational group for offending and non-offending adults. Parents who participate in this joining ritual are less angry and more co-operative when they begin individual or family therapy. They have an idea of the changes they would like to begin making. Therapy becomes a place where family members can escape their lifestyle of isolation and become a member of a group on a journey of change.

Identity Redefinition: Separation from normative rituals

Separation from old ideas, roles, and habits of interaction continues throughout the therapeutic process. During the course of treatment, adults who were molested as children separate from descriptions of themselves as powerless victims. As these individuals work toward a new description of themselves, they may reduce contact with family members and friends who are not supportive of the developing picture of themselves.

As the new picture becomes more clear, they may discover that they no longer fit into their old habits of being taken for granted and treated as unworthy or as not measuring up. During holiday times, participation in old rituals often invites a return to the old view of self as helpless and powerless. Creating new rituals:

.   solidifies the new picture persons are developing about themselves;
.   circulates this new picture to significant others; and
.   prevents people from being beckoned back to old family interactions

through participation in those old family rituals.

One young woman who had been molested by her father, did not want to give up participating in the holiday rituals of her family, but felt she could only handle limited exposure to her childhood home without being invited back into old interactions. She carried a small glass slipper to remind herself that she could only participate in the family 'ball' for so long without turning back into the family scrubgirl. She scheduled three two-hour visits, announcing at the beginning of each that she had to attend another engagement in two hours. Her off-times were spent with her 'Godmothers', friends that supported the new story about her as a person.

Children who have been removed from their parents' home and placed in foster care often struggle with beliefs about family loyalty. During holiday seasons, new rituals can be co-created with the child and foster parents that incorporate a favourite ritual from the child's family of origin. This helps children separate from the notion that they must choose loyalties to one family or the other. It also promotes a sense of inclusion and camaraderie within the foster home.

LIMINAL PHASE

In the rites of passage analogy, the liminal phase is a period of transition. The individual or family has separated from their old story or status, but have not yet developed or solidifed a new picture of self and relationships. There is a shift away from known ways of thinking and patterns of interaction, to experimentation with new thinking and behaviour. During this period of change, people often experience discomfort, confusion, and disorganization; everyday experiences are no longer predictable (Kobak & Waters 1984).

Disclosure of child sexual abuse and subsequent intervention by social control authorities, shatters the picture that family members have had about themselves and their relationships.

Scrutiny by child protection workers and law enforcement personnel often invites family members to intensify patterns of interaction that maintain denial. It is not uncommon for offending fathers to deny the occurrence of abuse, non-offending mothers to vacillate between believing the victim and supporting the offending parent's denial, or victims to recant their allegations (Summit 1983). Vicious cycles which maintain denial are intensified when family members experience helpers as insisting that they give up all of the beliefs and interactions that make up their sense of personal and shared identity.

The first task during the liminal stage of treatment is to help family members begin to experience the events subsequent to disclosure as opportunities for growth. Interventions are planned to help family members respond to the feelings of discomfort that prevail during the liminal phase with a sense of anticipation about possibilities for the future rather than with a return to interactional patterns that maintain denial.

To accomplish this, the therapist encourages family members to challenge their expectations about change and how it happens. Most often, these families view change as threatening. They expect change to be discontinuous and occur as the result of some cataclysmic event. Therapeutic rituals can assist family members in discovering the fluid and evolutionary nature of change.

The therapist can assist family members in discovering that they began to experience change long before the intervention by authorities. Disclosure would not have taken place if events were not occurring in the family that created readiness for change.

Readiness for change can be enhanced when family members are encouraged to identify positive and constructive aspects of their beliefs and relationships. When family members can be clear about what they don't want to change about themselves and relationships, it is much easier for them to redescribe feelings of discomfort during the liminal phase as anticipation about a future that will be different from the past.

Using ritual to develop an alternative story

Identity Redefinition: Escaping vicious cycles

A ritual based on the metaphor of a path has been used to help family members in understanding the evolutionary nature of change and identifying resources available to negotiate transitions. Family members are asked to draw a path which represents their journey from the past to the present. They are assisted in locating obstacles they have overcome and in identifying what they have learned about themselves in the process. These obstacles might include circular paths they have taken that represent the vicious cycles that create vulnerability to abuse. They are then asked to draw possible paths family members might take in the future. The future paths include many forks and branches going in a variety of directions. Family members might also be asked to speculate about the obstacles they might face should they choose a particular direction and how they might prepare to face those obstacles. They might be questioned about ways they have been able to escape the vicious cycles represented by the circular path and get back on a progressive course.

This ritual serves to create a view of change as fluid and ongoing. It also helps clients begin to identify the resources that have prepared them for change. Through the identification of obstacles, the ritual concretizes the restraints which have contributed to the maintenance of the problem. The view of a future with many potential directions punctuates the notion of choice. Most often, individuals from abusive families lack a sense of personal agency and perceive themselves as having few choices. In families whose patterns of interaction promote a shared identity at the expense of individual differences, the path metaphor can be used to punctuate uniqueness by examining the various paths family members might choose.

The ritual was originally developed by a team working with a fourteen year old girl. She had been placed in foster care when her mother refused to believe allegations she was being molested by her biological father. Subsequent to her foster placement, she began to get into fights at school. During the joining process, the therapist discovered that she enjoyed American Indian romance stories. She explained that she admired the women in the stories, as they had 'a lot of spunk'. They used this 'spunkiness' so that the men always thought they were in charge, when in reality the women were. 'Spunkiness' was externalized and questions were asked to help this young person discover how she could get 'spunkiness' to work for her and keep her out of fights or work against her so she would continue to get in trouble at school. The path ritual was used to help her identify situations that invited 'spunkiness' to create problems. Over the course of six sessions, she began to take charge of her spunkiness and use it to stand up for herself.

The path ritual has proven particularly helpful at times when persons who have chosen a new path find themselves back on the circular path. One young woman with a history of severe abuse experienced a number of relapses. She modified the path to help her solidify the developing alternative story about herself. She identified obstacles that invited her back to the old story about herself as a mental patient and wrote them on slips of paper that she placed at critical junctures on the path. She arranged the slips of paper so that she could lift up the description of the obstacles and find reminders to herself about ways she had successfully turned down previous invitations to get back on the circular path and return to the old story.

Dilemmas can be raised by asking family members questions regarding the consequences of choosing a particular path or life course. With one woman who was molested as a child, the path ritual was used to compare the different futures she could look forward to if she continued her current lifestyle of physical disability or embarked on a new path in the direction of health. Many adults who were molested as children have long psychiatric careers. The path ritual can also help these individuals choose between the lifestyle of a mental patient or the lifestyle of a 'survivor'. The future of a mental patient includes notions of chronicity. The description of 'survivor' includes a protest of victimization and an inevitable transition to a person whose identity is not defined by past exploitation.

When persons reach various decision points or crossroads, the path ritual can be re-enacted to assist them in choosing which direction to take. Decisions regarding reunification are often difficult for families to make. The path ritual can be used to help individuals gauge their readiness for reunification. If family members decide to reunify, the path ritual can be used to help anticipate the potential roadblocks that are inevitable as a consequence of changes individuals have made. The re-enactment of the ritual punctuates the process nature of experience and change.

Identity Redefinition: Punctuating resources

With one family, a storytelling ritual achieved many of the same objectives as the path ritual. This particular family had a long history of violence. The mother grew up in foster care and married a man who was physically abusive. She became clinically depressed following an accident in which a child in her care was killed. She made a decision to help her family escape violence when she overheard her husband and his mother discussing committing her to the state hospital and placing her children in foster care. The description of a 'pioneer' was offered to this woman by a supervision team because of her efforts to create a future for her children that was different from their abusive past. Her oldest sons were having particular difficulty escaping violence. She began to consider the obstacles she had overcome in her pioneering efforts, and to share stories about pioneers with her children. The stories that she told exemplified the lessons she had learned.

The ritual brought into sharp relief, the slow but steady progress this woman had made. This progress might have been lost in the ongoing crises associated with the physical and sexual abuse perpetrated by her sons. It also provided a perspective on relapse, as pioneers sometimes have to backtrack and consider alternative routes. The ritual helped to punctuate this woman's strengths and creativity. Through her stories, she was also able to punctuate her children's resources to overcome violence.

Identity Redefinition: Selecting out previously neglected aspects of lived experience.

Rituals can be developed to help children from extremely impoverished backgrounds select out exceptions to a view of self as 'damaged goods'. A tree metaphor was used in a ritual developed to assist a twelve year old girl with a history of sexual abuse who had been rejected by her biological parents, adopted parents, and several foster parents. In a conversation with her therapist, this young person described how much she enjoyed climbing trees. A graphic representation of a tree was used to help her escape the effects of abuse and abandonment. She labelled the roots of the tree with those aspects of herself that she appreciated. She identified people who had nurtured the tree to help it grow. Leaves that had fallen from the tree were labelled with those family beliefs and practices that she did not want to continue for herself. This ritual helped her identify more positive aspects of her lived experience. Shortly before the holiday season, she was placed for adoption. During her last therapy session, she and her therapist made Christmas ornaments representing her strengths. They placed the ornaments on a live tree that she took with her to her new home.

Belief Negotiation: Escaping restraining beliefs

During the liminal phase, family members are encouraged to examine the beliefs they espouse and determine if these ideas are relevant to their current stage in the life cycle. Of particular relevance are those beliefs that restrain change and contribute to vulnerability to sexual abuse.

One particular ritual co-evolved during a psychotherapy group for adults molested as children. The women in this group were struggling with old beliefs about themselves that they had acquired while growing up in homes where they experienced abuse. Beliefs such as 'my opinions don't count' or 'you can't trust your own experience' no longer fit for them, but continued to invite them back into a victim lifestyle. They agreed to return the next week with a list of those ideas which they experienced as disempowering. They discussed each belief, and decided which ideas they were ready to get rid of. One at a time, the group members then burned the slips of paper describing these beliefs. The following week, they decided to stage a wake for the loss of these ideas. Group members reported on changes they noticed since freeing themselves from these disempowering beliefs. A few weeks later they wrote birth announcements to proclaim the arrival of new beliefs that were more suited to them. Since that time, group members have shared this experience with new participants and burned other restraining ideas. Re-enacting the ritual has helped group members mark their progress over time.

Healing: Developing expectations for reciprocity

Variations of the odd days/even days ritual can be used to help clients examine beliefs that interfere with the development of reciprocity in relationships. As discussed above, women in abusive families often equate their personal worth with caretaking. Many abusive males believe that 'you have to get to give'. These ideas contribute to patterns of interaction where there is little give and take. These patterns may appear with regard to task functions, emotional intimacy, and sexual relationships.

A three stage ritual can be used to encourage couples to experiment with reciprocal interaction. This intervention was used with one couple presenting for marital difficulties related to the female partner's history of molestation. Both partners complained about their difficulty initiating emotional closeness, physical affection, or sexual intimacy. As the partners discussed their experience, the belief that 'you have to get to give' was externalized. The first stage of the intervention encouraged both partners to develop a repertoire of responses. This was accomplished by having each partner make a list and experiment with various behaviours. Partners also practised identifying whether they desired emotional closeness, physical closeness, or sexual contact. A variation of the odd days/even days ritual was introduced during the second stage of the intervention. Interactions defined as affectionate were identified from each partner's repertoire. Initiation of affectionate behaviours was to be carried out by one partner on odd days and the other partner on even days. In stage three the odd days/even days ritual was applied to initiation of behaviours from each partner's repertoire of sexual behaviours.

Healing: Escaping symptoms

Therapeutic rituals can also be devised to help clients escape the negative effects of abuse. Durrant (1987) argues that therapies which require re-experiencing of affect intensify the victim's experience of self as helpless and powerless. He believes that it is more healing for victims of child sexual abuse to use therapy to develop a sense that they are in charge of their feelings. They can then consider the emotional impact of sexual abuse without being overwhelmed by many and confusing feelings.

Rituals can be introduced to help children who have been victimized begin to experience a sense of control. Variations of fear busting (White 1986a) and temper taming (Durrant 1989; Epston 1989) activities are particularly effective in helping children escape symptoms that occur as a consequence of abuse. Children are encouraged to personify their symptoms by drawing a picture of them and giving them a name (e.g. 'touching monsters', 'scared person monsters', 'stealing monsters', etc.). When they have performed individualized monster taming activities, the pictures are placed in a box which serves as a collective repository for monsters that create problems for children. The box is secured with a chain and padlock. As part of their growing competence, children who have tamed monsters are given the combination to the lock. The collective nature of this ritual reduces isolation and instills hope. Through participating in the ritual, young people learn that other children have been sexually abused. They also discover that these children have been able to escape the fears and troubles they experienced as a consequence of abuse.

Healing: Overcoming victimization and loss

A formal apology from the offender to the victim is a ritual that does much to promote healing (Trepper 1986). This therapeutic ritual requires extensive preparation. Over the course of several sessions, offending and non-offending parents are encouraged to examine a number of issues including:
- ideas or interactions which made their family vulnerable to experiencing abuse;
- what they have done to change these concerns and what they plan to continue to accomplish;
- what information to share with their children given their various stages of development; and
- how they will respond if they become aware that the child is experiencing sexual exploitation in the future.

During this same period of time, the therapist works with the children to gauge their readiness. The children are encouraged to write questions for their parents to consider. These questions assist parents in developing an understanding of the victim's experience of exploitation.

After revision, a formal apology session is scheduled. This ritual is designed to relieve the children of any feelings of responsibility they might have for the abuse. The parents answer the children's questions and share their resolve to create a different future. They are encouraged to collapse time forward and consider how their family will be different given their escape from secrecy. They might be encouraged to consider the ways that family members will continue to change and what they will be like when they complete therapy. They might be asked to consider ways the next generation will be different as a consequence of their intervention and resolve to overcome abuse. Some form of penance for the offender might be arranged as part of the apology ritual.

REAGGREGATION PHASE

In the reaggregation, or reincorporation phase, of a rite of passage, the new stories developed by family members are circulated to significant persons. Sharing the story helps solidify changes family members have made as a consequence of participation in therapy. When the new story is performed for an 'audience', new beliefs and interactions become part of lived experience. Feedback provided by the audience can be drawn on to maintain the new story. The new story is recognized by members of the community, who begin to interact in ways consistent with the new status the person has achieved (Koback & Waters 1984; White & Epston 1989). One young woman who was molested as a child arranged a series of 'coming out parties', where she symbolically declared to significant persons in her life that she was coming out of hiding and recognizing herself as a person of worth and talent.

Circulating the new story

A variety of contexts provide opportunities for circulating the new story to an audience. A 'catching up ritual' has been used in therapy groups for adults molested as children and mothers of child victims to celebrate and circulate the many small steps that members have taken. Each time a new person joins the group, members share with other participants the most recent changes they have taken that are pleasing to themselves. The beginnings of the new story are circulated and new members are invited to participate in its development. The ritual creates a tone of hope rather than despair.

Rituals can be devised for use in therapy sessions to help family members reincorporate the new descriptions of themselves. A continuous collage has been used to document change over the course of treatment. Family members begin by creating a collage that represents the story about their family at the time of disclosure. As therapy progresses, additional sheets of paper are added to the original collage which depict changes family members have made. The new description is concretized through the construction of the collage. The re-enactment of the ritual illustrates that change is a continuous process. At the end of therapy, the collage is presented to the family with instructions that they are to continue to use the collage to record future changes in their life story.

Family members solidify and circulate new stories about themselves and their relationships by serving as consultants to persons who are beginning the process of separation from archaic beliefs and interactions (White & Epston 1989). Persons who have completed therapy groups for offending and non-offending parents return as consultants to describe the details of their journey from their status at disclosure to their status in the present. The arrival of the new story can be historicized by videotaping presentations for use by other persons beginning the journey. The tape serves as a counter document that is created to affirm the presenter's new status. The tape can be reviewed by the presenter should s/he be invited back into the beliefs and interactions that contributed to the old story. When children or adult 'survivors' are under the influence of the effects of abuse, consultants can offer valuable ideas about how to challenge such effects.

When family members are involved with multiple helpers, it is important to catch up members of the larger system on changes which family members are making. It is helpful for family members to invite helpers from protective services, school, the court, and other groups at critical junctures during treatment for updating on family or individual changes. When professionals do not notice or acknowledge change, family members can be invited back to a view of themselves as victimized by the larger system. Feedback from professionals about changes family members are making helps to promote responsibility and to solidify developing beliefs and patterns of interaction.

Circulation of the new story outside of the therapeutic realm is an important aspect of the reincorporation phase and is especially critical for family members who have been disempowered by secrecy and isolation. Affiliation with non-problem oriented groups provides opportunities to experiment with new behaviours. A context is created for persons to separate from the role of 'client' and perform their new story for a different audience. Lived experience is developed apart from the experience of abuse and victimization.

Maintenance rituals

During times of high stress, persons who have developed alternative and more empowering stories about themselves remain vulnerable to the return of the oppressive dominant story. Certain circumstances might also be associated with risk for relapse. Rituals can be devised to help people minimize setbacks and maintain their new view of self and relationships.

'Walking on eggshells' is a frequent description of the experience of living in a family characterized by abuse. One mother whose daughter had been sexually assaulted used these words to describe the interaction in her home. She explained that her husband had 'terrorized' the family. He would abuse alcohol and/or drugs on a regular basis. When under the influence of these substances, he would drive the family car in a dangerous manner or invite other people to fight with him. From the mother's description, a 'shell lifestyle' was externalized. Prior to disclosure, the mother had invested all her energy keeping people outside of the 'shell' from knowing what was happening inside. The beliefs and interactions that contributed to a 'shell lifestyle' were mapped. The mother held many beliefs about family loyalty and became concerned that to achieve change she would have to abandon all of her values. At this point, the mother was asked to consider the ways these values could work for her or against her. She was invited to consider the benefits of choosing a 'cocoon lifestyle'. A cocoon provides a place of safe refuge from the outside world. The description of a cocoon also includes expectations that the occupant will experience a metamorphosis and venture into the outside world.

At termination, this metaphor evolved into a ritual designed to help maintain changes family members had made. During the session, each family member identified the steps they had taken in the development of the new story. Each step was recorded on individual slips of paper. These descriptions were stored in egg shaped containers. Family members could access these descriptions during those times when they were vulnerable to returning to the old story. As family members took additional steps, descriptions of those new steps were added to the container.

Celebration

Celebrations are often planned to punctuate reincorporation. The celebration provides a context where the new status the individual has achieved is recognized by others. Certificates or trophies may be awarded to solidify accomplishments.

Latency age girls who participate in a psychotherapy group have planned 'escape from secrecy' parties to celebrate their success in escaping the effects of abuse. Several weeks are spent preparing for the occasion. Decisions are made about who to invite to the party. Girls have chosen to invite family, friends, foster parents, and therapists. Skits and puppet shows have been created to catch up guests on the protection and problem-solving skills they learned in group. Posters and other decorations were made to symbolize their escape from secrecy and abuse. During the celebrations, the 'gossip' game was played to illustrate how secrets contribute to confusion and breakdown in communication. In this childhood game, a whispered 'secret' is passed from person to person in the room. The girls and their guests were then separated into two groups. Each group developed a list of how the girls had changed since their escape from secrecy. The groups were reunited and their lists were read aloud. Next, the girls and their guests watched videotapes depicting what the girls had learned through their participation in group. Finally, trophies proclaiming their escape from secrecy were awarded.

The escape from secrecy party served to:
- redescribe the girls in terms of their strengths,
- promote healing and escape from the effects of the abuse, and
- circulate this new story of strength to significant persons.

Similar celebrations have been developed for other age groups. The metaphor of story has also been used. Children have considered the characteristics of heroes that they exhibited in challenging abuse: they were **brave** enough to tell someone about the abuse, **courageous** enough to come to group for the first time, and **strong** enough to stand up to the effects of abuse. A celebration was planned around these aspects of being heroes of their life story. Day long celebrations have been planned for adults who were molested as children. Participants have used their creativity to reclaim their lives from abuse through dance movement, poetry, short stories, and painting. Too often, disclosure of child sexual abuse involves a situation characterized by guilt and shame. These celebrations create a context that punctuates competence and worth.

CONCLUSION

Traditional conceptualizations describe families who have experienced incest as among the most 'resistant to change'. A cybernetic conceptualization views family members as 'restrained' by oppressive dominant stories that arrest changes that are necessary for development across the life cycle. Change is restrained by:

• beliefs that interfere with the development of a sense of personhood, and

• vicious cycles that perpetuate denial of lived experiences, promote isolation, and encourage a shared identity at the expense of individual growth.

Interventions are designed to empower family members to challenge restraining beliefs and interactions and develop stories about their lives and relationships that are not dominated by abuse and victimization.

The ritual process facilitates change by creating a sense of security and stability. Rituals can be designed to help family members identify those aspects of lived experience they want to continue to embrace. The use of ritual challenges family members' negative views of changes by placing them in charge of direction and rate at which change occurs. Personal agency is facilitated because family members learn to recognize and celebrate the many small steps they take. This appreciation of the evolutionary nature of change assists family members in:

• separating from those aspects of lived experience that are no longer viable and

• experimenting with new beliefs and behaviours. Rituals provide an opportunity for family members to celebrate change and circulate their new story to the larger community.

NOTES

1. Trepper & Barrett (1986, 1989) have introduced the notion of vulnerability to intrafamily child sexual abuse. These authors discuss vulnerability within the context of a diathesis-stress model. Incest is assumed to occur when:
   • a combination of individual, family, and environmental factors combine to create vulnerability;
   • the family experiences a precipitating event; and
   • resources for coping are depleted. The ideas introduced by these authors provide a useful model for assessment and intervention in child sexual abuse. The current conceptualization applies the notion of vulnerability within the context of cybernetic theory. This model is not concerned with the causal notions

considered in a diathesis-stress conceptualization. Cybernetic theory assumes that problems develop as a result of random events or chance occurrences that:
- are interpreted within the context of an oppressive dominant story;
- contribute to restraints; and
- prevent family members choosing solutions that are more viable for the problem at hand.

ACKNOWLEDGEMENTS

We gratefully acknowledge the special assistance of our colleague, Patricia Sterne, who participated in the co-creation of a number of these rituals. Acknowledgements are also extended to: Nona Hutton, for elaborating on the joining ritual which externalizes vulnerability to intrafamily child sexual abuse; Beth Persac, for modifying White's fear busting ritual to include a collective repository for 'bad monsters'; and Lyn Lucas, for her comments on an earlier draft of this chapter.

REFERENCES

Alexander, P.C. 1985:
   'A systems theory conceptualization of incest.' **Family Process**, 24:79-88.
Barrett, M.J., Sykes, C. & Byrnes, W. 1986:
   'A systemic model for the treatment of intrafamily child sexual abuse.' In Trepper, T.S. & Barrett, M.J. (Eds.) **Treating Incest: A multiple systems perspective**. New York, Haworth Press.
Durrant, M. 1989:
   'Temper taming: an approach to children's temper problems revisited.' **Dulwich Centre Newsletter**, 3-11.
Durrant, M. 1987:
   'Therapy with young people who have been the victims of sexual assault.' **Family Therapy Case Studies**, 2(1):57-63.
Epston, D. 1989:
   'Temper tantrum parties: saving face, losing face, or going off your face.' **Dulwich Centre Newsletter**, p.12-26.
Finklehor, D. 1986:
   'Abusers: special topics.' In Finklehor, D. (Ed.) **A Sourcebook on Child Sexual Abuse**. Beverly Hills, California, Sage Publications.
Gelinas, D. 1986:
   'Unexpected resources in treating incest families.' In Karpel, M.A. (Ed.) **Family Resources**. New York, The Guilford Press.
Gondalf, E.W. 1985:
   Men Who Batter. Holmes Beach, FA, Learning Publications.
Hoke, S.L., Sykes, C. & Winn, M. 1989:
   'Systemic/strategic interventions targeting denial in the incestuous family.' **Journal of Strategic & Systemic Therapies**, 8(4):44-51.
Imber-Black, E., Roberts, J. & Whiting, R. (Eds.) 1988:
   Rituals In Families and Family Therapy. New York, W.W. Norton.
Imber-Black, E. 1988:
   'Ritual themes in families and family therapy.' In Imber-Black, E., Roberts, J. & Whiting, R. (Eds.) **Rituals In Families and Family Therapy**. New York, W.W. Norton.
Jenkins, A. 1987:
   'Engaging the male incest perpetrator.' **Dulwich Centre Newsletter**, p.15-16.

Koback, R. & Waters, D. 1984:
  'Family therapy as a rite of passage: play's the thing.' **Family Process**, 23:89-100.
Kowalski, K. & Durrant, M. 1989:
  'Sexual abuse: assisting a transition from victim to person.' Workshop presented at the meeting of the **American Association of Marriage and Family Therapy** (October), San Francisco, California.
Roberts, J. 1988:
  'Setting the frame: definition, functions, and typology of rituals.' In Imber-Black, E., Roberts, J. & Whiting, R. (Eds.) **Rituals in Families and Family Therapy**. New York, W.W. Norton.
Selvini Palazzoli, M., Boscolo, L., Cecchin, G. & Prata, G. 1977:
  'Family rituals: a powerful tool in family therapy.' **Family Process**, 16:445-453.
Selvini Palazzoli, M., Boscolo, L., Cecchin, G. & Prata, G. 1978:
  'A ritualized prescription in family therapy: odd days and even days.' **Journal of Marriage & Family Counselling**, 4:3-9.
Straus, M., Gelles, R. & Steinmetz, S. 1981:
  Behind Closed Doors: Violence in the American family. New York, Anchor Books.
Summit, R. 1983:
  'The child sexual abuse accommodation syndrome.' **Child Abuse and Neglect**, 7:177-193.
Tomm, K. 1989:
  'Externalizing the problem and internalizing personal agency.' **Journal of Strategic & Systemic Therapies**, 8(2):5-9.
Tomm, K. 1984:
  'One perspective on the Milan systemic approach: Part II. Description of session format, interviewing style and interventions.' **Journal of Marital & Family Therapy**, 10(3):253-271.
Trepper, T.S. 1986:
  'The apology session.' In Trepper, T.S. & Barrett, M.J. (Eds.) **Treating Incest: A multiple systems perspective**. New York, Haworth Press.
Trepper, T.S. & Barrett, M.J. 1986:
  'Vulnerability to incest: a framework for assessment.' In Trepper, T.S. & Barrett, M.J. (Eds.) **Treating Incest: A multiple systems perspective**. New York, Haworth Press.
Trepper, T.S. & Barrett, M.J. 1989:
  Systemic Treatment of Incest: A therapeutic handbook. New York, Bruner/Mazel.
White, M. 1986(a):
  'Anorexia nervosa: a cybernetic approach.' In Elka-Harkaway, J. (Ed.) **Eating Disorders and Family Therapy**. New York, Aspen.
White, M. 1986(b):
  'The conjoint therapy of men who are violent and the women with whom they live.' **Dulwich Centre Newsletter**, Spring.
White, M. 1986(c):
  'Fear busting & monster taming: an approach to the fears of young children.' **Dulwich Centre Review**, p.29-34.
White, M. 1986(d):
  'Negative explanation, restraint & double description: a template for family therapy.' **Family Process**, 25:168-184.
White, M. 1986(e):
  'Ritual of inclusion: an approach to extreme uncontrolled behaviour of children and young adolescents.' **Dulwich Centre Review**.
White, M. 1987:
  'Family therapy & schizophrenia: addressing the in-the-corner lifestyle.' **Dulwich Centre Newsletter**, p.14-21.

White, M. 1988(a):
'The process of questioning: a therapy of literary merit.'**Dulwich Centre Newsletter**, p.8-14.
White, M. 1988(b):
'Saying hullo again: the incorporation of the lost relationship in the resolution of grief.'**Dulwich Centre Newsletter**, p.7-11.
White, M. 1988/89:
'The externalizing of the problem.'**Dulwich Centre Newsletter**, Summer.
White, M. & Epston, D. 1989:
Literate Means to Therapeutic Ends. Adelaide, Dulwich Centre Publications.

CHAPTER III

OVERCOMING THE EFFECTS
of
SEXUAL ABUSE:

Developing a self-perception
of competence

by

Michael Durrant
&
Kate Kowalski

The field of therapy with people who have been sexually assaulted is replete with prescriptions for clients and therapists alike. With the increased awareness of the incidence of sexual assault has emerged a plethora of ideas about the effects of abuse, the 'damage' caused by abuse, and what children and adults 'need' to do in order to recover from this damage. Such ideas have led to the emergence of a new breed of professionals. Many of us 'ordinary' therapists are discovering that we have clients with whom we can work concerning their behavioural or emotional problems; however, they need to see a 'sexual assault counsellor' in order to work on the specific issues related to the experience of abuse.

The seriousness of the issue of sexual abuse and our increased awareness of the number of people who have lived large parts of their lives secretly oppressed by their memories of their experience of abuse, is perhaps one of the things that leads therapists to want to 'get it right' in working with these clients. Thus it is not surprising that we crave some expertise to guide us in our endeavours. In thinking about therapy with victims of sexual abuse, we have been concerned about the unintended consequences of our growing expertise in this area and the increasing notion that sexual assault therapy is somehow a different, or more difficult, or more specialised area of therapy.

THINKING ABOUT THE THERAPEUTIC CONTEXT

Some years ago, our colleague, David Epston (1984), proposed a schema for thinking about therapies, in which he contrasted 'therapies of degradation' (or 'missionary therapies') with 'therapies of regrading' (or 'anthropological therapies'). The former category included therapeutic approaches founded on the therapist's 'knowledge' about what was best for the client and so sought somehow to lead the client to that point. Epston's concern was that, even if this therapy was successful in resolving the presenting difficulties, the context it established could easily become one of clients having had to submit to the power and expertise of the therapist. Hence, even the client who apparently ended therapy successfully may be considered, paradoxically, to have emerged from the process with lesser status. The latter category, on the other hand, suggested an approach that was more co-operative and believed that clients could have a major influence over the direction in which therapy progressed and in defining what it was that was helpful for them.

We have found Epston's schema helpful in thinking about our own work in the area of sexual abuse. Influenced by White's ideas about people's self-description, we have proposed a variation of Epston's paradigm (see below).

Therapy which promotes a self-perception as 'victim'	Therapy which enhances a self-perception as 'competent person'
1. Therapist is expert ... has special knowledge regarding sexual abuse to which client needs to submit.	1. Client as expert in her/his own life ... has ability to determine what is best for her/him. Therapist respects this.
2. Client is viewed as damaged or broken by the abuse.	2. Client is viewed as oppressed by and struggling with the effects of the abuse.
3. Deficit model ... seeks to 'fix' client.	3. Resource model ... seeks to build on strengths and resources of the client.
4. Insight into dynamics of the abuse is key goal of treatment.	4. Goal of treatment is client viewing him/herself as competent and as having control over the influence of the effects of the abuse.
5. A cathartic or corrective experience is necessary to produce change.	5. Best 'corrective experience' is client getting on with his/her life in a way which best suits him/her, and change will be promoted by experiencing this possibility.

Table 1: A schema for thinking about therapeutic approaches

The schema encourages us to consider the context established by the experience of the process of therapy, as well as the way that context compares with the experience of the abuse itself. Much has been written about the persistence of a sense of helplessness and incompetence being one of the effects of abuse. Our concern has been whether the experience of therapy establishes a context within which clients may experience themselves as competent, versus one in which, even if difficulties seem to be 'resolved' or 'worked through', clients do not experience the process of therapy as one in which they exercised and experienced competence.

A context of 'victimhood' vs competence

Central to this concern is a consideration about the notion of being a 'victim'. We are clear that our clients who have been sexually assaulted were victims of a violent and oppressive act, over which they had no control and in which they in no way colluded, nor invited. Given the fact that children may experience feelings of guilt, shame or blame, it may be important for their 'innocence' or 'victimness' to be communicated. However, we remain concerned that some clients continue to have the idea of being a victim as a central part of their view of self.

The Shorter Oxford Dictionary (Little, Fowler & Coulson 1973) offers the following definition of victim: *one who is reduced or destined to suffer under some oppressive or destructive agency.* The notion of being 'destined to suffer' clearly implies an ongoing nature of the state of being a victim, and we suspect that this is similar to popular notions of being a victim. That is, people may continue to see themselves as victims and so have an ongoing view of self that precludes the possibility of experiencing competence or confidence. A number of clients have commented that they expect to suffer emotional and/or interpersonal difficulties later in life, as if this were inevitable, and the spectre of such difficulties becomes a kind of Sword of Damocles overshadowing any life experiences which might otherwise promote ideas of competence, health or satisfaction with life. Thus, such concerns may act to become a self-fulfilling prophecy, which encourages the occurrence of further difficulties through the process of clients being more likely to interpret events in terms of the abuse, rather than in terms of developmental and other life pressures which might be overcome[1]. Thus, we have considered approaches to therapy which reinforce the definition of self in terms of victimhood, wherein the client continues to 'have' the quality or characteristic of victimhood, in contrast to approaches which serve to enhance a definition of self in terms of ongoing competence.

Intrinsic to those approaches which promote a continued self-definition as a victim are concepts of the (almost) inevitable damage or disturbance that sexual assault creates. As White & Epston (1989) have suggested, therapies based on metaphors of damage or breakage are essentially deficit models. The implications of a deficit model is that someone (the therapist) must identify the damage and its causes, and is then in a position to know what steps are necessary for the client to undertake in order to remedy this damage. The process of the therapy relies on the 'expert knowledge' of the therapist about abuse and its effects and treatment, and a belief in such knowledge easily leads to definitive statements about essential components of treatment. As therapists who have spoken with many clients who have been sexually assaulted, many of us have gleaned ideas about some of the things that a number of our clients have found helpful. Such information clearly is useful in our attempts to interact helpfully with other clients. Unfortunately, it is only a small step from there to the point at which we believe that clients **must** go through particular steps or experiences, so that our observations about what many clients find helpful become normative. For example:

Victims must be helped to get in touch with their repressed rage and to express anger in a healthy and non-destructive fashion. (Porter, Blick & Sgroi 1982, p.121)

The process of then leading our clients through these 'required' steps or processes is inevitably one of imposition of ideas about what is helpful or necessary[2]. It may well be that a number of clients find the steps or process that is thus prescribed to be helpful; nonetheless, the context in which it occurs can easily be one of submission. It may be that such submission is voluntary (although the pressures of the legal and mental health systems may lead to such volition being illusory), as opposed to the experience of assault in which submission was involuntary, however the parallels are striking. We have felt increasingly uncomfortable with a stance that requires clients to submit to our prescription of their experience and have come to view such a process as oppressive and as potentially perpetuating the effects on self-view of the abuse itself.

Adapting Epston's schema, we have considered approaches to therapy which serve to enhance a view of self that centres on experiences of competence. In considering such approaches, we suggest that it is not only the content of the therapeutic process that may encourage such a view of self, but the context within which it develops - a context that includes the stance of the therapist vis a vis the client and the client's experience of their own agency in the process and outcome. Essential to such a process is a stance which suggests that the client's views about what is helpful are more salient than the therapist's beliefs about what is therapeutic, and we acknowledge that this is a stance that is contradictory with much of our training as therapists. However, it is not sufficient, in our view, to adopt an understanding, sympathetic, even empowering, stance if the therapy then pursued entails, implicitly or explicitly, a therapist dictating what it is through which the client must go. Our experience with many clients suggests to us that our clients know best, and that beginning from this premise has a profound effect on the direction and 'tone' of the therapeutic encounter.

Resources and solution vs deficit and problem

A therapy which promotes a view of self as a competent person is essentially a resource model, rather than a deficit model. It suggests not that abuse creates some damage or disturbance, but that the experience of abuse effects the client's self-view in such a way as to mask or obscure those events and experiences which might form the foundation for a self-definition of competence. From this view flows an approach that seeks to build upon strengths and resources, rather than correct or rectify damage or deficit.

In considering the two categories of therapy suggested above, one might also describe the distinction as being that between a problem-focused (or past-focused) approach, and a solution-focused approach.

Problem-focused (or problem-oriented) approaches have gained some prominence in the medical and mental health fields. Such approaches are grounded in the task of achieving as complete a list of problems as possible. The search for such a list may result in a formidable compilation of issues to be addressed:

Compiling a complete problem list can only be accomplished by collection of a comprehensive data base. Identifying and listing all of the problems helps, in turn, to focus the intervention and treatment plan... It is extremely helpful to utilize a preformulated list of problem categories in order to make the problem list as complete as possible. (Sgroi 1982, p.87)

An approach that is problem-focused has the risk of allowing the problem to continue in a person's (view of) life. White (1989) offers the notion of the 'problem saturated' view of self that clients hold, whereby their view of the problem becomes the lens through which they see themselves and the world. We suggest that a problem-focused approach to therapy may contribute to the persistence of such a problem-saturated view, paradoxically even if the problem appears to have been resolved.

A solution-focus, on the other hand, seeks to encourage clients to develop what we might term a solution-saturated view of self (and a view of future possibilities) - one in which the solution and its achievement replaces the problem as the lens through which life is viewed.

It should be noted here that our concern with problem-focused approaches is really a concern with **past** problem-focused approaches. That is, 'problem-solving' approaches, particularly the brief therapy approach of the Mental Research Institute (MRI) (Weakland et al 1974), are similarly concerned with avoiding pathologizing and with changing current patterns of thinking and acting, and so might be seen to have a focus on things being different in the future. Such approaches may be problem-focused, however, they include an implicit orientation towards future rather than past, and so do not lead to therapy that is 'problem-dominated'.

MAIN PRINCIPLES OF OUR APPROACH

Our work has been influenced by the solution-focused approach of de Shazer (1985, 1986, 1988), as well as the restraints and narrative ideas of White (1986, 1989).

de Shazer and his colleagues, at the Brief Family Therapy Center (BFTC) in Milwaukee, developed their approach based on Milton Erickson's ideas about people's resources, and with the influence of Bateson. The solution-focused approach evolved from the Milwaukee team's early thinking and experimenting with strategic and systemic approaches such as those of MRI, Haley and the Milan team. Their work led them away from a problem focus to solution construction with clients when they recognised that what clients found helpful ('solutions') often appeared to the therapist to have no direct relationship to the problems presented, but in some way 'fitted' with the client's unique experience (de Shazer 1985). As a result, the emphasis of treatment shifted from the therapist trying to understand the problem and how to help clients solve it, to asking clients questions and prescribing tasks to help them focus on their own perception of needs and goals and their own existing and potential resources for solutions (Lipchik 1987; Molnar & de Shazer 1987). As part of this process, they 'discovered' the notion of **Exceptions** - finding that asking clients about times the problem wasn't a problem (or was less so) seemed more helpful than asking about the times it was a problem. The solution-focused approach has continued to develop, at BFTC and elsewhere, by exploring different ways to identify and build upon exceptions.

White's initial work was grounded in Bateson's notion of restraints - those beliefs and ideas that make it less likely that people will notice those events and aspects of their experience that are at variance with the problem-saturated description they hold. White proposed forms of questioning which sought to challenge the influence of such restraints and open space for the recognition of other aspects of experience. Whilst we see White's approach as essentially a problem-focused approach, his framework has been helpful in offering ways to talk about problems that may create a platform from which solutions may be identified.

From our consideration of these two influences, and our experiences with clients, we have proposed a set of principles or assumptions that guide our work with clients who have been sexually assaulted (see Table 2). These are essentially statements of belief, or a philosophical stance, upon which we base our approach.

Fundamental to these principles, and to our approach, is a distinction between 'the abuse' and 'the **effects** of the abuse'. Clients attend therapy, not because they have been abused, but because they are experiencing some personal or relationship difficulty (which may well have had its genesis in the experience of abuse). Their own beliefs about the origin of their difficulty may lead to their seeing the abuse as the problem, nonetheless it is the ongoing difficulties which they wish to have resolved: *The incest survivor who comes to therapy brings with her not only the predicament of dealing with past abuse, but also the repercussions of the abuse that may be causing difficulties in her current life. (Dolan 1989, p.3)*

That is, the abuse is only a problem because of its effects. This distinction, though perhaps semantic, is important. Therapy which seeks to resolve the abuse is inevitably problem-focused and easily leads to the characteristics that we have described as constituting a therapy which promotes a view of self as victim. Since the abuse cannot ever be made to have not happened, a problem defined as the abuse can never truly be resolved. Therapy which focuses on the effects of the abuse may encourage a solution-focus, since it is easier to imagine that specific, ongoing effects

PRINCIPLES OF THERAPY
WITH THE EFFECTS OF SEXUAL ABUSE

1. Sexual abuse does not **inevitably** lead to emotional or psychological problems. In spite of having experienced something quite painful and confusing, people who have been abused have many strengths and resources with which to solve difficulties.

2. It is more helpful to consider, 'what keeps this problem alive in this person's life, and keeps it from being resolved?' (a focus on context/restraints) rather than, 'what caused this problem?' (leads to examination of family dynamics, individual pathology, etc.).

3. One of the main effects of sexual abuse is the assault it makes on the person's self-perception. As the abuse can blind people from noticing their strengths and capabilities, they develop an 'abuse-dominated' view of self and interaction.

4. People inadvertently notice and place greater emphasis on 'facts' which support the abuse-dominated descriptions of themselves, others, relationships, and situations. People unwittingly co-operate with the 'life' or 'career' of the effects of the abuse, due to the incremental nature of problem development.

5. Complex problems like sexual abuse don't necessarily require complex solutions.

6. Every abuse-dominated pattern includes examples of EXCEPTIONS which serve as hints towards solution. Focusing on these small 'chinks' in the client's behaviour or self-perception can serve as a foundation upon which she can build a new view of herself as competent and in-control.

7. The client's difficulties need to be defined and talked about in a way which helps her/him feel optimistic about and effective in resolving them.

8. The goal of therapy is to assist the client in overcoming the effects of the abuse and to make sense of her/himself and the experience in a way which frees her/him to live a satisfying life, rather than to help the client 'work through' the abuse.

9. In order for effective changes to occur, the person first has to see her/himself through a lens of 'competence' rather than 'incompetence', 'in-controlness' rather than 'out-of-controlness', 'self-respect' rather than 'self-hate', 'forgiveness' rather than 'self-blame', etc.

10. It is not necessary to directly discuss details of the abuse in order to diminish the effects. Clients are the best judges of whether, and when, it is helpful to discuss the abuse explicitly.

TABLE 2: Principles that guide our work.

may be able to be resolved or overcome. As we have suggested previously (Durrant 1987), we acknowledge that clients were victims of abuse, however, we suggest that they may be able to not remain victims of the ongoing effects of the abuse.

Sexual abuse does not inevitably lead to emotional or psychological problems. In spite of having experienced something quite painful and confusing, people who have been abused have many strengths and resources with which to solve difficulties.

The statement that sexual abuse does not inevitably lead to emotional or psychological problems, in no way suggests that we should view sexual abuse in a more benign manner. Rather, it is a statement that the **effects** of an experience of abuse may be ameliorated by a number of factors, not the least of which may be therapy. As Trepper & Barrett (1989) suggest:

The belief that [sexual abuse] will lead to severe emotional problems has been the cornerstone of all therapy ... Most therapists probably believe this without hesitation, and probably justify some of their more intrusive therapeutic measures on it. The research on the long-term effects of child sexual abuse has been quite mixed, however ... (p.11)

Many of us who work in this arena will be acutely aware that a number of factors may exacerbate the effects of abuse, including the ways in which family members, friends and professionals respond at the time of disclosure. Either way, we find it helpful to recognise the effects that may (and may often) be associated with sexual abuse, but to see these as not being inevitable. In keeping with our suggestions above, we have found that it is often the self-fulfilling assumption of this inevitability which, in itself, leads to ongoing problems. If clients, or therapists, believe that difficulties are inevitable, then any therapeutic intervention occurs within a context of virtual futility. It is not surprising that some clients take the view that the best for which they can hope is to develop the ability to 'cope' with the pain and difficulties that they will carry with them for ever.

An earlier paper (Durrant 1987) related the case of a young man who had been sexually assaulted at age nine, and, when seen in therapy five years later, was quite clear that he would grow up to be a sexual offender. The certainty with which he held this view made it not surprising that he was unable to experience himself as able to exercise control over his present behavioural difficulties, which were seen by others as sexual behaviours indicative of unresolved trauma, and by himself as bizarre. However, the more he was able to experience himself as having some control over these effects of abuse, the more he was able to entertain the possibility of his future being different.

It is more helpful to consider, 'what keeps this problem alive in this person's life, and keeps it from being resolved?' (a focus on context/restraints) rather than 'what caused this problem?' (leads to examination of family dynamics, individual pathology, etc.)

A focus on effects, and the idea that the domination of these is not inevitable, leads to a consideration of what is obstructing or restraining solution, rather than what is causing the problem. A problem/abuse focus requires that we dig, and uncover the causes of the problem (what we might term the 'archeological' approach to therapy), and thus therapy proceeds from an identification of pathology - whether that pathology be framed in terms of intrapsychic conflict, dysfunctional family interaction, and so on. Utilising Bateson's idea of negative explanation and restraints, we may focus on the factors in clients' views, or beliefs, that acted to prevent the possibility of change (White 1986). Our focus on resources (and hence solutions), assumes that change is constant and is the natural occurrence, therefore problems represent something getting in the way of these being recognised and/or acted upon. A focus on overcoming whatever is getting in the way presents quite a different task to one of identifying and resolving whatever caused the problem in the first place. This is in keeping with the distinction between the abuse itself and the ongoing effects, since we might assume that the ongoing effects are kept going by the operation of certain restraints that get in the way of clients feeling that they can overcome them.

A focus on restraints leads us to look not only at those ideas and beliefs that operate for the individual and which encourage a self-perception that allows the effects of abuse to dominate, but also to those societal and cultural expectations, prescriptions and beliefs which reinforce certain aspects of a person's experience or self-perception. Such cultural restraints create a climate within which a person who has been sexually abused is more likely to develop an abuse-dominated, or self-deprecating, view of self. For example, there are many societal and cultural prescriptions for the experience of women which serve to promote a sense of incompetence, powerlessness, and a feeling of responsibility. Such restraints establish a 'bias' for the selection and interpretation of information, and make it more likely that women will interpret the effects of abuse as representing some deficit or fault on their part.

One of the main effects of sexual abuse is the assault it makes on the person's self-perception. As the abuse can blind people from noticing their strengths and capabilities, they develop an 'abuse-dominated' view of self and interaction.

A focus on restraints and context is essentially a focus on meaning. In line with the recently espoused 'constructivist' approaches (Watzlawick 1984), we have a basic assumption that people are engaged in a constant process of making sense of their experience. The uniqueness of people's experience means that it is the sense they make of events that lead to their behavioural and emotional responses, not the events themselves. In his recent work, White has employed the 'text' or narrative analogy to describe the ongoing way in which people construct an explanation for their experience. One might see this in terms of the persistent self-perception that the individual holds, or personal constructs (Kelly 1963). The individual's self-perception provides a template against which experiene and events are interpreted, and determines what aspects of their experience will be noticeable or salient to them. Hence, the meanings ascribed to events and the experience of events operate to filter the available information about self. The operation of such restraints or self-perception serves to perpetuate patterns of behaviour, or emotion, by not allowing the individual access to the possibility of alternatives.

It follows that we may consider one of the main effects of sexual abuse to be the assault it makes on the person's self-perception.

People inadvertently notice and place greater emphasis on 'facts' which support the abuse-dominated descriptions of themselves, others, relationships, and situations. People unwittingly co-operate with the 'life' or 'career' of the effects of the abuse due to the incremental nature of problem development.

We may assume that the experience of being abused is such a powerful experience, which may arouse powerful feelings and reactions, that it establishes a context that begins to permeate the process of thinking about self and the world. Following White's notion that people develop a 'problem-saturated' self-description, we suggest that people develop an 'abuse-dominated' view of themselves and their interactions. Their experience of abuse, and the way they make sense of it and its effects, become a sort of 'lens' through which the rest of their experience is viewed.

Usually, people inadvertently notice, and place greater emphasis on, facts which support the abuse-dominated view of themselves, others, relationships and situations. The lens of the abuse-dominated description means that they are more likely to interpret their own (and others') behaviour and emotions in ways that fit with this view. So, the experience of helplessness may promote a self-perception dominated by this feeling, which makes it likely that further events will act to reinforce feelings of helplessness. Thus, people may have a growing sense of their inability to overcome their particular difficulties. They may even behave in ways that, to we professionals, seem to exacerbate their difficulties, since their behaviour will be consistent with the abuse-dominated view they hold. [Therapists are familiar with the notion that people's 'attempted solutions' to problems, which are reflections of their view of the problem and of their own abilities to do something about it, often inadvertently lead to their actually doing 'more of the same'. (Watzlawick et al 1974)]

Complex problems like sexual abuse don't necessarily require complex solutions.

In the light of the seriousness of the problem of having been abused and the assault it makes on people's lives and view of self, it is not surprising that many of our clients feel totally overwhelmed and believe there is nothing they can do to improve their lives. It is also easy for therapists to find the prospect of seeking to assist in a process of change to be overwhelming in the face of what appear insurmountable odds. We find it essential in our work to hold the view that complex problems (such as the effects of sexual abuse) do not necessarily require complex solutions. We do not wish to understate the magnitude of people's difficulties, nor the multi-faceted nature of the development of their present view of life and self. Nonetheless, we are concerned that the therapeutic endeavour should be seen, and described, in a way that gives it a chance! A problem-focus brings with it the weight of the complexity and enormity of the origin and development of the problem. A solution-focus recognises that solutions may begin with small changes on which larger changes may be built.

As therapists, we have available to us many metaphors for describing problems and building treatment approaches (and whatever way we choose to make sense of the problems with which clients present, our frameworks are no more than analogies or metaphors), and some metaphors make therapy more complicated and tortuous than others without necessarily making it more likely to be successful. Moreover, de Shazer and his colleagues discovered from their experience, with a variety of clients, that the things which clients reported to be helpful in moving towards a solution did not necessarily appear to bear much relationship to the problem. Notwithstanding any protestations that such clients were not **really** having lives as successful as they now experienced them, or that the solutions were somehow illusory, the fact remains that clients sometimes find simple things helpful (one may only assume that our clients have not had the comprehensive training that we have undergone in how to complicate matters!). A solution-focus has enabled us to embrace non-complex solutions for seemingly complex difficulties.

Every abuse-dominated pattern includes examples of EXCEPTIONS which serve as hints towards solution. Focusing on these small 'chinks' in the client's behaviour or self-perception can serve as a foundation upon which she can build a new view of herself as competent and in-control.

One of the key principles of Erickson's work was that of **utilization,** which he defined as:

... utilizing a patient's own mental processes in ways that are outside of his usual range of intentional or voluntary control. (Erickson, Rossi & Rossi 1976, p.19)

Erickson's assumption was that there were at least parts of a person's mental processes that could lead towards a solution, and that the utilization of these was more beneficial than the use of a direction imposed by the therapist. That is, people have resources, however they often are unaware of them. Building on this idea, solution-focused therapy rests on the assumption that there will always be exceptions to a problem pattern, that there will be times or situations in which the problem is not a problem, or is less of a problem, and that these provide the foundation for solution-development.

White (1988) has employed a similar idea in speaking of 'unique outcomes'. He suggests that there will be aspects of a client's experience that do not fit with the evolving story that person has, and so will be unavailable to be made sense of. He suggests that these unique outcomes provide the raw material for a process of questioning that invites clients to build a new self-description or fashion a new story of their experience. White comments that the terms 'exceptions' and 'unique outcomes' are interchangeable, although we feel that it is not necessarily helpful to see such events as 'unique' or 'one-off' occurrences. Our experience is that there are many exceptions to problem patterns, however the abuse-dominated self-perception obscures these from clients' awareness.

According to Bateson:

For the benefit of stability, they pay the price of rigidity, living, as all human beings must, in an enormously complex network of mutually supporting presuppositions ... change will require various sorts of relaxation or contradiction within the system of presuppositions. (1980, p.158-159)

The abuse-dominated self-perception is that matrix of mutually supporting presuppositions within which all information and events are interpreted, and we might see these exceptions as the contradictions which might be utilised in building a view of a competent self.

The client's difficulties need to be defined and talked about in a way which helps her/him feel optimistic about and effective in resolving them.

A focus on exceptions need not necessarily lead to a therapy that ignores the clients' experience of the problem - and we would stress the importance of our clients feeling heard and understood. Nonetheless, a solution focus (which includes a focus on exceptions occurring now, and in the future, non-abuse-dominated state) may inject a more optimistic climate for therapy. Our experience is that a focus on effects rather than on the abuse itself, and an interview that tends towards talking about successes rather than analysing difficulties, allows clients to feel more optimistic as they begin to become aware of the real possibility of solution.

The goal of therapy is to assist the client in overcoming the effects of the abuse and to make sense of her/himself and the experience in a way which frees her/him to live a satisfying life, rather than to help the client 'work through' the abuse.

Thus, our goal in therapy is not seen in terms of assisting our clients to 'work through' the abuse, but rather to allow our clients to make sense of themselves in a way that is freeing. Whilst an overt focus on exceptions to abuse-dominated thoughts, feelings and behaviour may appear to be simply a focus on 'surface' behaviour, the target of therapy is the self-perception that has allowed, and been encouraged by, the ongoing difficulties.

In order for effective changes to occur, the person first has to see her/himself through a lens of 'competence' rather than 'incompetence', 'in-controlness' rather than 'out-of-controlness', 'self-respect' rather than 'self-hate', 'forgiveness' rather than 'self-blame', etc.

Overcoming the effects of abuse entails the client developing an alternate lens through which to interpret self, behaviour and interaction. Such a different lens allows the client access to resources and successes that were previously unavailable. That is, a client who views self through a lens of 'competence' is more likely to attend to examples of competent behaviour which will serve to strengthen that emerging view than is a client who views self in terms of incompetence. A client who looks through a lens of 'controlness' rather than 'out-of-controlness' is more likely to feel able to exercise control over previously overwhelming feelings or behaviours. A client who comes to view self in terms of 'self-respect' instead of 'self-blame' is more likely to be able to utilize those aspects of behaviour and experience that point to worthwhileness.

It is not necessary to discuss details of the abuse directly in order to diminish the effects. Clients are the best judges of whether, and when, it is helpful to discuss the abuse explicitly.

It flows from the above that it is not necessarily necessary to talk about the details of the abuse itself in order to promote solution. Our assumption is that the experience of behaving and interacting differently, and the process of making sense of these differences in a manner so as to develop a new self-perception, may result in discussing the details of the abuse being irrelevant. In a solution-focused therapy, lengthy discussion of the problem may not need to be part of the process. On the other hand, some clients will find that discussing the abuse itself is, in itself, an exception to their abuse-dominated view. We will discuss below the ways we consider these options, and the ways we invite clients to be the judges of whether or not it is helpful.

From these principles, we may summarise our view of the effects of abuse and a therapy which proceeds from that view, as shown in Figure 1.

A FRAMEWORK FOR THERAPY

We have developed a framework for therapy which is solution-focused, but also influenced by White's ideas about problems. Given that solution focus orientation sees therapy in terms of solution development rather than problem resolution, it follows that it is incompatible to punctuate the world of therapeutic endeavour by problem type. Increasingly, we find meaningless ideas such as 'therapy with encopresis', 'therapy with substance abuse', 'therapy with depression', and so on. The fact that solutions may bear little apparent relationship to the particular problem, and the stress on the uniqueness of each client's experience and self-perception, suggests to us that grouping clients or therapies, according to problem type, is a recipe for being prescriptive. As mentioned above, this appears to be a particular danger when one defines a special therapeutic arena that is 'therapy with sexual abuse'. Accordingly, we prefer to think of therapy as a process of identifying events and experiences that point towards solutions for a particular client's distress in a particular situation, and seeking to assist the client to form a new self-perception by building on these. Our general framework for therapy is outlined in greater detail elsewhere (Kowalski & Durrant, in preparation). Nonetheless, we acknowledge that groups of our clients share some common experiences and that we may illustrate our approach with examples drawn from a particular client constellation. Accordingly, we will elaborate our framework with particular attention to our own experiences in working with clients who have been sexually abused, and to the things they have told us about what they experience as helpful. The framework, focusing as it does on solutions and new meanings rather than on the category of problem, may

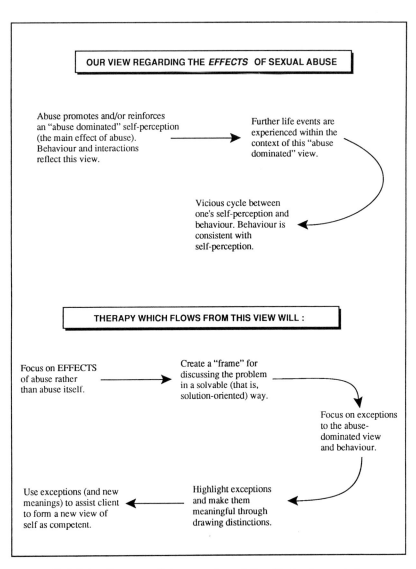

FIGURE 1: Conceptualising our view of the effects of sexual abuse, and of a therapy that proceeds from that view.

be employed equally usefully with related client groups, such as the mothers of adolescents who have been abused (Kowalski 1987).

Setting the agenda.

We have learned not to make assumptions about what it is the client wishes to have different in her life, so we begin by inviting our clients to set the agenda for therapy. Of course, this agenda may be at variance from that prescribed by the referrer.

An initial period of socialising or joining is particularly important with clients who may be hesitant about therapy, or who may have expectations of therapy that lead them to be cautious. It is often the case that clients who have been sexually abused have already had to talk to a number of medical, legal and welfare professionals, and are hesitant about yet another encounter, and such a period may yield valuable information about strengths, activities or resources that may form the basis for a later discussion of exceptions. Following from this, we seek to establish a context for therapy that will promote trust and a sense of co-operation. This may entail such questions as:

- *What is it that you think it would be helpful for me to know about your situation?* or

- *What do you think it would be best for us to talk about today?* or

- *I've heard from (the welfare department) some information about what has happened to you, but I wonder what things you think are important for me to know?*

Colleagues of de Shazer comment that they have heard him say that 'clients determine what we talk about ... therapists determine how we talk about it', and we consider this an important stance to take.

Some clients will nominate the experience of abuse specifically as the subject matter for therapy, whilst others will express more immediate concerns such as, 'my daughter and I haven't been getting on well since this all came out' or 'I feel so depressed and hopeless all the time', etc.

As part of setting the agenda, we seek to introduce a solution focus as early as possible, inviting clients not only to state what it is that is the problem, but also what types of things will constitute the solution state. It can be helpful to begin an interview with a question such as:

How will you know when you don't have to come here any more? (Lipchik 1988, p.107)

Such a question is loaded with suggestion - it implies that there will be a time when therapy is no longer necessary; it implies that the client will be the judge of when this time is; and it implies that the client has some access to, or ability to imagine, that time now. We have found similar questions to be useful, such as:

- *Let's imagine that your coming here and our talking together turns out to be helpful, what do you think you will notice that is different? (or ... how will you know?)*

Such questions make it clear that clients are setting the agenda for what it is **they** wish to achieve. Moreover, they invite clients to specify actual events, experiences or behaviours that will characterise the solution state and we will encourage clients to be as specific as possible. Questions such as:

- *What do you think you will be doing differently when that happens?* or
- *So, how will that make a difference for you?* or
- *What do you think you will notice about yourself, or find yourself doing, that will tell you that things are better?*

are helpful, as may be questions that invite small examples, such as: 'What do you think will be the first thing you will notice yourself doing that will tell you that things are better for you?'

Fit between what the therapist does and what the client wants is crucial - no matter how skillful a therapist may be, all is lost if the therapist is proceeding in a direction or talking in ways that do not fit the client's experience and desire for change. One of the factors that promotes promotes such 'fit' is when ... *goals are established to help determine how the client and therapist alike will know when the problem is solved. (de Shazer 1988, p.93)*

CASE EXAMPLE 1 - Kate Kowalski

Jackie, 23, was referred by the director of the area sexual assault service after contacting the service to enquire into receiving counselling. Jackie explained that, as a child, she had been sexually abused by her father over the course of several years and that she was concerned that current relationship difficulties might be related to this experience. When the sexual assault director made the referral, she said she felt that Jackie had never really 'worked through' the abuse and that it was her impression that this would be necessary in order for Jackie to deal with her concerns about the current relationship.

When Jackie came for therapy, I explained that I had spoken with the sexual assault counsellor and relayed what she had told me about Jackie's situation. I then asked a question which I quite routinely ask clients where someone else has provided information: 'This is what the counsellor told me about your situation, but what do you think is most helpful for me to know?' With this, Jackie explained that she was engaged to be married to a very nice man with whom she had been involved for the past two years. She was quite happy with the relationship and felt it to be 'the real thing'. However, she was concerned that recently she was feeling increasingly jealous in social situations that involved her fiance and her women friends. This was most upsetting to her because she trusted him and her friends, and felt that their interactions really had not warranted the jealousy she was feeling. Jackie found herself wondering recently whether this jealousy was in some way connected to the abuse she experienced as a child. She wasn't sure exactly what the connection would be, but, because she thought her recent concern was exaggerated, was beginning to worry that perhaps she really hadn't 'dealt with' her history of abuse.

In order to establish a context for proceeding in a way that would be most suited to Jackie's concerns, I asked several questions to set the agenda. These included: 'Let's assume that our getting together and talking ends up being helpful to you, how will you know?' 'What will be happening differently for you?' 'What will be a small sign to you that things are getting better for you?' 'What do you suppose your fiance will notice that will let him know that you're feeling more relaxed?' All of Jackie's responses related quite directly to her relationship. She responded with statements such as: 'I'll feel less jealous.' 'I won't get so worried with we're out with our friends and John talks with one of my girlfriends.' 'I'll be able to go out and relax again.' 'John will notice that I just seem to be having more fun. I won't be asking so many questions about whether or not he really loves me. I'll just believe it when he tells me, because he does tell me.'

I was interested that Jackie's responses to the agenda-setting questions were all related to her relationship with John and not directly related to her concerns over the past abuse. Given her clarity about what would be different, I decided to proceed by asking questions which would indicate whether any part of these identified 'goals' was already happening now or in the recent past, and to set aside any direct discussion of the abuse. This proved fruitful as Jackie was able to identify a number of incidents in which she was already behaving and feeling in a way which was consistent with her desired state. As we discussed these 'exceptions', she began to experience herself as more 'relaxed', 'confident', and 'sure of myself'.

In a subsequent session, I asked Jackie about her previous concern about the abuse. As she was generally feeling more confident and self-assured, she said she truly felt that she had dealt with what her father did quite effectively. This led to a discussion of the steps Jackie took to bring the abuse to an end, as well as the fact that, years later as an adult, she told him very clearly that it was he who was wrong and that she had no intention of blaming herself for his behaviour. She said she still thought about it occasionally, but basically felt that talking about it would not really change things a great deal.

The problem with talking about the problem.

Sometimes the agenda-setting questions provide an opening for immediately moving on to exploring exceptions, but this is not always the case. As we have said, we do not believe that a solution-focus precludes any discussion of the problem. In fact, the problem with not talking about the problem is that clients may feel unheard, and as if their experience of distress is being disqualified. On the other hand, since talking is the way in which views of reality are maintained and promoted (Berger & Luckmann 1966), we might suggest that the problem with talking about the problem is that it may make the problem bigger. That is, the process of 'rehearsing' the effects of the abuse may strengthen the perception of the enormity of the difficulty, or may enhance the abuse-dominated view.

Family therapists are familiar with the notion of 'reframing' problems - redescribing problems in such a way as to give them a different meaning (Watzlawick et al 1974, p.95, for example). De Shazer (1988) suggests that it is particularly when a client views the problem within a 'global frame' that he or she may find it difficult to identify and/or acknowledge exceptions which might not fit with that view (p.101). Such global frames are not uncommon with clients who have suffered such a huge assault on their self-perception as have those who have been sexually abused. They may adopt self-perceptions that are not framed in terms of specific problems - such as, 'I have difficulty getting to sleep at night.' or 'I find myself having outbursts of rage.' - but are framed as global statements about the essential nature of self - such as, 'I am worthless, I feel like dirt' or 'I am unable to control my sexuality'. Clearly, to launch into: 'so tell me about a time that you didn't feel like dirt', would be to take a large risk of being seen as insensitive and having not understood how bad things are.

It is in such situations that we find it essential to discuss the problem, but to seek to do so in ways that redefine or reframe it in a solvable manner. White's notion of externalizing the problem (1984, 1988/89) is a form of reframing that we find particularly helpful in such situations. Externalizing the problem entails reframing, or redescribing, the problem in a way that suggests it as some entity outside the person, to draw a distinction between person and problem. Rather than the problem being viewed as a part of the person (consistent with ideas about emotional damage), it may be considered **as if** it were something distinct that is somehow affecting and dominating the person. As Tomm (1989) points out, the fact that a person might be able to consider themselves as 'facing' a problem, rather than 'being' or 'having' a problem, may enhance the possibility that they can entertain ideas of having some agency over the problem. This distinction between person and problem is consistent with the distinction we have drawn between the abuse and its effects, since many people who have been sexually abused tend to see themselves as the problem, rather than being able to identify the effects of abuse as leading to the difficulties.

Externalizing the problem (White 1988/89) offers a way of overcoming the objectification of persons that traditional diagnostic formulations impose. The fact of being sexually assaulted may be an 'objectifying' experience for the person. Many common ideas about abuse and its effects similarly promote the objectification of persons (and their bodies). Such objectification both tends to offer prescriptions for people's experience, and makes the possibility of solution seem more removed. Externalizing the problem seeks to counter this by objectifying the problem (the effects of abuse) rather than the person.

Externalizing the effects of sexual abuse may entail the process that White refers to as 'relative influence questioning', in which the client is asked about the influence of the problem (the effects of the abuse) in her life, and which sets the stage for asking about the influence she has been able to have over the problem. In keeping with ideas of 'fit', it is important that the particular words used to describe the externalized problem are consistent with the client's own language. Whilst therapists may be familiar with externalized 'names' for other problems that involve some element of the fantastic (such as 'Sneaky Poo' or 'The Temper Monster'), such terms are likely to appear flippant when applied to the effects of abuse. Moreover, as Durrant (1989) suggests, it is the **process** of externalizing that is more important than the **name** given to the externalized problem, and the name used may actually change as therapy progresses. We prefer, at least at first, to use or adapt the client's own language in describing the problem.

Having asked agenda-setting questions, our client may have replied with global responses such as: 'I want to feel better.' or 'I won't be so depressed.' We may follow such replies with questions that seek to understand the impact of the effects of the abuse, whilst at the same time beginning to suggest an externalized description.

- *How has the problem been a problem in your life?*
- *In what way has feeling bad had an effect on you/your life?*
- *In what way/s is depression still getting in the way of things you want to do?*
- *In what way/s has feeling awful kept you from moving forward in a way you would like?*
- *In what way/s have you noticed this guilt getting in the way of your life?*
- *How much has what happened to you influenced your life? How much do you think it has held you back?*
- *In what ways have your memories and thoughts about what ..... did got in the way of you moving forward in your life?*
- *Were there ways that the memories tried to stop you talking about them?*

Externalizing the problem in this way begins to establish a platform on which the identification of exceptions may be built. As White (1988/89) states:

In assisting [clients] to separate themselves and their relationships from the problem, externalization opened up possibilities for them to describe themselves, each other, and their relationships, from a new and non-problem-saturated perspective... From this new perspective, persons were able to locate 'facts' about their lives and relationships that could not even be dimly perceived in the problem-saturated account; ... facts that provided the nuclei for the generation of new stories. (p.3)

CASE EXAMPLE 2 - Kate Kowalski

Michelle, a 22 year old university student, was referred by a local family service agency after an attempted sexual assault in her home in which she fought off the assailant. She appeared for counselling several weeks after the assault, complaining of persistent fears and anxiety attacks. She explained that she had been prone to bouts of anxiety which had been worse lately. She attributed this both to the assault as well as to the increased pressure and demands of her studies.

As Michelle explained what led her to seek counselling, focusing primarily on the anxiety, I began to ask questions in a way which sought to imply an externalized description. Questions such as: 'How has the anxiety been getting in the way for you lately?' 'What effect has the anxiety been having on you?' 'How much has the assault fuelled the anxiety?' 'What kinds of things has the anxiety got you worrying about lately?' were interspersed with comments which also served to reinforce the externalized frame. This portion of the interview was meant to understand the influence of anxiety and fears in Michelle's life, and as a prelude to being able to punctuate the ways in which she was currently standing up to the problem's influence.

Michelle talked about the ways the anxiety encouraged her to worry about her mental state and, in particular, had her questioning whether she was going crazy. It had her focusing more and more attention on it, thereby leaving little room for her to think about other things (i.e. her studies, having fun, going out with friends, etc.). The anxiety was also working hard to convince her that maybe she really couldn't handle university and should consider dropping out and moving back to live with her parents. It also had her parents considering much the same thing. In general, the anxiety was taking up increasing amounts of Michelle's time, thinking and energy, and was encouraging her to question herself.

Continuing to use the externalized description, I invited Michelle to consider times when she had not succumbed to the anxiety's pressure, times when the anxiety could have got the better of her, but did not, and times when she prevented it from overwhelming her. She seemed to find these types of questions a bit difficult at first, but then went on to give a number of examples of times she was able to keep the anxiety at bay. This then led to a discussion of what was different about these times, as well as how recalling and appreciating these examples as significant made a difference to Michelle's view of herself. This style of interviewing continued over the course of the five sessions we met, with Michelle reporting in the final session that she felt much more at ease, stronger, and in control of the anxiety.

Identifying exceptions to abuse-dominated behaviour and feelings.

As mentioned above, exceptions to abuse-dominated feelings and behaviour provide the foundation for the development of solutions. Particularly if clients have given fairly specific responses to agenda-setting questions, the search for exceptions may proceed directly, without needing to embark upon the process of externalizing, or otherwise redefining.

For example, the client who begins by saying: 'I feel so self-conscious and embarrassed that I can't talk to people', and who identifies the solution-state as involving: 'I guess I'll be able to talk about myself a bit without bursting into tears or having to change the subject', might be invited to speculate on the exception that exists here in the session: 'From what you've said, it must have been pretty difficult to come along today, knowing that you might have to talk about yourself. How do you think you've been able to do that so far?'

On other occasions, exception questions will proceed naturally from externalizing the effects and questions about their impact. In either case, the aim is to invite the client to identify times when the problem could have been a problem but wasn't, or wasn't as much.

- *Tell me about a time when you were even a little successful in standing up to the problem.*
- *Was there a time when things were even a little better? What was different then?*
- *Was there a time recently when feeling awful could have got the better of you, but you did something to prevent it? What did you do?*
- *Can you recall a time when the depression seemed to be taking charge, maybe tried to stop you doing something you wanted to do, but you did something to take charge yourself? What did you do?*
- *Can you think of a time when the effects of the abuse were exerting their strength, but you were able to prevent them from overtaking you? How*

did you do that?

- *Which time stands out for you as the one where you really stood up to the influence the problem wanted to have on your life? How did you do it?*
- *It seems like there have been ways that you stood up to what was done to you and didn't allow the memories and feelings to have their way with you completely. Do you think that telling people about them was a further step in getting back control of your life away from them?*
- *Are there ways you have been able to not allow your feelings of guilt to cripple you?*

It is useful to ask clients to be as specific as possible about such exceptions, and to describe them in detail. Questions such as: 'So, can you think of a **particular** time when you were feeling better?' 'Tell me more about the most recent time that happened.' 'Tell me more about what you did differently', and so on, may be useful. It does not matter how small the exception is, it is the fact of its identification that is important.

CASE EXAMPLE 3 - Kate Kowalski

Karen, a 32 year old single, professional actress, was referred for counselling a few weeks after being sexually assaulted by an acquaintance. In the initial interview Karen explained how the assault had been affecting her, primarily that it had her thinking more and more about her history of feeling exploited and taken advantage of in relationships. She felt that in each relationship in which she had been involved, she had 'lost' herself and had basically become the person her partner wanted her to be. In discussing this pattern over the course of the first two sessions, it became clear to Karen that this was the case, not only in intimate relationships, but within her family relationships as well.

During the second meeting, I introduced the idea that Karen seemed to have developed a pattern of 'living her life according to other people's wishes' and feeling bad at those times when she was 'living life according to her own wishes'. This way of framing the difficulty seemed to fit Karen's view and allowed a description of the desired solution to evolve. That is, Karen said she would know that things were different for her when she was 'living my life according to my own rules rather than everyone else's'. When asked to elaborate on what this would mean for her, Karen replied that she would be saying 'no' to her mother more often when demands and expectations were placed upon her, she would be standing up for herself in disagreement with more confidence, and she would be more openly expressing her views in social situations, rather than quietly sitting back and worrying that what she had to say might offend someone.

I was curious to know whether Karen could identify any times when she was already living her life according to her own rules, even in very small ways. I was convinced those times existed (based on a number of things Karen shared about her work and about her interactions with her mother, with whom she was currently living), but was interested in whether Karen would recognize anything. Questions such as: 'Was there a time recently when you could have given in and done what someone else wanted you to do, but did what you wanted instead?' 'When was the last time someone had ideas about what you should do, but you were able to maintain your own ideas?' 'When was the last time you said 'no' to your mother?' and 'What's different about those times when you're able to do what you know to be right for you, rather than giving in to what someone else thinks would be best?' were asked in order to invite Karen to consider herself in a new way and begin to build a new view of herself as someone who, in fact, can (and does) live life according to what she knows to be best for her.

Karen readily offered a number of examples where, within the last several weeks, she resisted the temptation to give in to other people's prescriptions for her. Several of these situations involved her mother and older brother, both of whom had very strong negative opinions about her choice of an acting career. Her mother had been trying to convince her that she should give up acting and go into a more 'stable and secure' line of work, while her brother would frequently telephone from his home interstate and encourage Karen to reconsider her options. Still, while Karen had some concerns about her career, particularly the options available to her in the city in which she was currently living, she was very clear that acting was the thing she found most rewarding. I expressed interest in the fact that, in spite of the past coaching she had received in 'living life according to other people's expectations', she was able to be so clear of her chosen career path and asked how she accounted for this. Karen seemed a bit taken aback by this and seemed to find it interesting as well, replying: 'I never thought of it that way. Maybe I'm better at standing up for myself than I thought I was.' I was also interested in the other things she identified as evidence of 'living life according to what I know to be right'.

We continued, over the next several sessions, to explore these exceptions and highlight them in relation to how this information made a difference to Karen's view of herself. At one of our later meetings, Karen told me of her plan to move to another city, one that would increase her career options and open up more creative possibilities. This was especially interesting in that her mother found this very difficult and actively tried to discourage Karen from considering the move. Karen was able to appreciate her strength in not succumbing to her mother's disapproval and found her ability to do this pleasing. She was still concerned about her mother's feelings about the move, and was now much more able to hear what her mother had to say without feeling like she had to give in to her mother's desires. In fact, as Karen came to view herself as more 'my own person', the easier she found it to be open and compassionate with her mother because she no longer feared her mother would convince her to do something she really didn't want to do.

Inviting clients to entertain ideas of personal agency or competence - making exceptions meaningful.

Exceptions to abuse-dominated feelings and actions may not immediately seem meaningful to clients. In the face of a self-perception grounded on the experience of helplessness, hopelessness, and incompetence, it is not surprising that clients will often attribute experiences or events that we regard as exceptions as being due to external factors. That is, they may identify a particular situation in which things were better (they were not so depressed; they were able to achieve things previously beyond them; and so on), but are likely to hold the view that they played no real part in the occurrence. Given that the abuse-dominated self-perception provides a lens that denies the possibility of competence, such clients may assert that things were better because their partner did something different, their children were more co-operative, their employer or teacher was more understanding, and so on.

It is important not to attempt to convince clients that exceptions are significant. Attempting to convince often amounts to an irresistible invitation to argue even more strongly for the abuse-dominated view. Rather, we find it helpful to adopt a stance of curiosity and ask questions that invite clients to entertain ideas of personal agency. Essentially, such questions take the form of:

- *How do you account for this?*
- *What do you think you were doing to contribute to this event?*
- *How do you account for your ability to do this?*
- *Is this something that surprised you about yourself ... the fact that you were able to stand up to the depression in this way?*
- *What about you helped you to be able to do this?*
- *Did you know before you told your Mum about what your Dad did to you that you would be able to do it? How did you know that about yourself?*
- *What was different about this situation compared with one when the problem was more in charge? What was different about you?*
- *It seems like this might have been a time when you've shown that you can be your own person rather than being pushed around by what other people want, as if you were their property. That sounds like a pretty big step. How do you think you were able to do it?*
- *I'm interested that you were even able to consider doing something for yourself rather than just for other people. I'm wondering how you think you were even able to imagine yourself doing this.*

Our aim is not that clients should have a sudden realisation about their competence. Whilst comments such as: 'I've never really thought about it like that', are not uncommon, we might expect that the strength of the abuse-dominated self-perception will make it difficult for them to appreciate their own part in exceptional events. In many ways, the process is one of gentle persistence, raising questions, inviting speculation, and planting seeds.

Inviting clients to build a new view of self: self perception questions.

Having identified exceptions and questioned in ways that invite speculation on the client having done something different, our aim is that these differences begin to be connected in a way as to suggest a new view of self. The approach of the BFTC team concentrates on identifying and amplifying exceptional events, and he maintains that clients appear to begin to see their future, and its possibilities, differently such that they decide they no longer require therapy. It is clear that de Shazer's approach is concerned with the 'reality' constructed by therapist and client and that the outcome of therapy is related to the creation of a more solution-focused reality. However, he does not seem to intervene directly at the level of clients' view of self, believing that the experience of solution behaviours (and their personal and interpersonal consequences) will inevitably affect the client's 'reality'. White (1988), on the other hand, is quite overt in his attempts to participate with clients in the recasting of their self-perception (or the 'writing of their new story', as he would describe it (p.12).

It is our experience that, as clients are able to attend to those aspects of their behaviour and emotion that are exceptions to their seemingly persistent complaint, and to speculate on their own part in achieving these, they begin to see their future more hopefully. This increased hopefulness may become self-amplifying, as it counteracts the effects of the abuse-dominated view of self and sets a context for the noticing of continued exceptions. As such, it has implications for a more competent self-perception. However, we are also aware that the experience of abuse, and of coping with the feelings associated with that experience, tends to promote an abuse-dominated self-perception that is persistent; and that the process of building a new view is not a simple one. In many ways, we might think of the process of identifying exceptions and focusing on personal agency as a process of **deconstructing** the prevailing view of self. White's interventions around clients' self-description offer a way of beginning the process of **reconstructing** self-perception.

White (1988) suggests categories of questions that he terms 'unique redescription' and 'unique possibility' questions which might also be termed 'self-description' and 'circulation' questions. These questions invite clients to speculate more directly on the implications of their 'discoveries' for their view of self and for their view of others' view of them. The questions take the general form of: 'What does this tell you about yourself?' although they must be framed in language that is meaningful for the particular client and fits with his/her situation:

- *So what do these things tell you about yourself that the feelings had been hiding from you?*
- *Can you see why the fact that you managed to stand up to the guilt in this way makes me think you are pretty strong?*
- *What do you think the depression would have found out about you from this?*
- *So what would Mum have learned about you from this?*
- *What do you think your teacher has noticed about you that is different?*

What ideas might this give him/her about you? Are there ways you can help him/her keep having this idea about you?

- *Did you know this about you before or is it something new?*

CASE EXAMPLE 4 - Michael Durrant

Susan, 17, had recently disclosed that she had been sexually abused by her grandfather for a number of years from the age of 8. She described how she had felt trapped by his continued presence and by the secret she carried, and how she continued to feel guilty about her feelings about him, in the face of her family's view of him as gentle and caring. During her early teens, she had attempted to cope with her situation by keeping away from him as much as possible, only to be the subject of rebukes from her parents in terms of: 'Why are you so rude to Grandpa?' 'You never seem to be worried about your homework, but you always manage to have some pressing work to do whenever we decide to visit your grandparents', and so on.

She described how her feelings of guilt and worthlessness had preoccupied her throughout high school, reflected in poor grades, few friends, and uncomfortableness about meeting boys. Her feelings of hopelessness and worthlessness had permeated everything, so she saw her poor school performance as a failure and her lack of friends as indicating that she was not a very nice person. Her disclosure had resulted from a particular teacher taking an interest in Susan and cultivating a friendship with her, initially designed to encourage her with schoolwork.

Susan had been taken to see a psychiatrist who had pressured her to recount the details of the abuse. She had not wanted to do this and refused to return to see him. The welfare authorities were concerned that she was somehow denying the abuse and referred her to our centre. Susan was obviously hesitant about therapy and anxious about what she might be asked.

Susan found it hard to respond to the early agenda-setting questions, unable to imagine what it would be like when things were better for her, and spoke generally about not feeling so awful, being able to concentrate on something else, and not feeling totally useless. However, she added that she could not imagine a time when she would be able to do anything well or when other people would think she was worth having as a friend. It also seemed that she found this line of questioning somewhat unexpected.

Given the general nature of the frame that she presented, I asked a number of questions about the effects of the experience on her, incorporating some suggestion of externalizing. Questions included: 'How much do you think your memories of what your grandfather did have got in the way of your life? What sorts of things have the memories got in the way of you doing?' and 'What are some of the ways that guilt has pushed you around and interfered in your life?' When asked about exceptions, Susan was not able to think of any times things had been different. To the question, 'Do you think that telling someone about this, after all these years, was a time you stood up to the memories and didn't let them decide what you were going to do?' she replied, 'Maybe. But I wish I'd never said anything; it's just made things worse. When I see what Mum and Dad are going through I feel worse - more guilty.'

It was clear that one of the effects of the abuse for Susan was that she had no confidence in herself or her ability to know what was right. I commented, 'I'm interested in the fact that you were strong enough to have some clear ideas about what was right for you', to which she replied that she didn't understand. 'Well, everyone else was telling you that you needed to talk about what happened to you, even the psychiatrist, but you knew that that wasn't what you needed. How do you think you were able to have such a clear idea about what you wanted and needed?' Susan wasn't sure, however this line of questioning clearly set her thinking, and she even joked with me about how arguing with psychiatrists can be pretty difficult. We discussed this exception for some time and I wondered about whether her feelings of hopelessness would have been very happy with her having such a clear idea about herself.

To a general question about what this told her about herself, Susan was unsure but commented that she 'had never thought about it that way'. She agreed that people might be able to see this as an example of her standing up for herself, something she had not thought she was capable of doing, and we speculated about what it might be like if she was able to think about herself that way.

Returning to her disclosure, I wondered if 'even though telling people about what happened has made things more difficult, do you think maybe that doing that was another example of standing up to the guilt?' and Susan recounted at length all the thoughts that had led to her disclosure. We contrasted this with the ways that the memories had tried to keep her quiet *over the years, and I posed questions about how she had been able to defy them in this way.*

As Susan began to entertain ideas that she had done some things for herself, she and I focused more explicitly on her self-perception. Questions about what these exceptions told her yielded some ideas about herself as more decisive or as stronger, however she appeared still to be dominated by feelings of lack of self worth. An exception to her view that other people considered her useless was the fact that her teacher had considered her worth making some effort to establish a friendship, and this provided the material for a series of questions about what things her teacher might have noticed about Susan that gave her the idea that she was worth getting close to. The process of encouraging Susan to identify those things about herself that her teacher might have thought valuable was long, however Susan was able to identify some characteristics of herself that were at variance with her abuse-dominated view. As we discussed what difference it might make to her if she was able to see herself more in the manner that her teacher saw her, Susan began to be more optimistic and further exceptions emerged on which she could build.

Future orientation.

Whereas a problem-focused approach points back to the past, a solution-focused approach is inherently future-oriented. It is grounded in the idea that there will be a time when the effects of the abuse are no longer dominating. It can be helpful to invite clients explicitly to focus on the future and consider how the discoveries they are making might make a difference.

In the interview, an explicit future orientation may be used both around future exceptions and around future self-perception.

A number of therapists have suggested approaches to questioning that include an orientation towards the future (for example, Lipchik 1988; Penn 1985; Tomm 1987). O'Hanlon & Weiner-Davis define 'future oriented questions' as being where 'clients are asked to envision a future without the problem and describe what that looks like' and suggest that 'the mere act of constructing a vision of the solution acts as a catalyst for bringing it about' (1989, p.106). In many ways, the discussion of exceptions is already future oriented in that the early agenda-setting and exception questions invite an imagining of life without the problem. Later in the therapy process, the future orientation may be even more explicit as clients are asked what sorts of things will be happening differently as they are able to build on the exceptions.

- *So, let's imagine that you will be able to do that again sometime, to do something that is not what the depression normally lets you do, how do you think that will make things different?*
- *How confident are you that you could do something like that again? What will it be like when you do? How do you think Mum will react when she notices you doing it?*

Future-oriented questions may also be useful in the session during the process of identifying exceptions, particularly if the therapist is not able to gain a clear picture about the effects of the abuse that are most pressing at the moment for the client. The archetypal question that might be employed is 'the miracle question', which takes the general form of:

- *Suppose that one night, while you were asleep, there was a miracle and this problem was solved. How would you know? What would be different? How will your husband know, without your saying a word to him? (de Shazer 1988, p.5)*

Questions of this type invite an imagining of the future solution state and may be used to gain information about particular behaviours that will be occurring. The therapist may then ask about times that any such things are already happening, or things that are indicative of some move towards their happening.

CASE EXAMPLE 5 - Kate Kowalski

In a role-play interview as part of a workshop at our centre, two sexual abuse counsellors role-played a mother and daughter, a few weeks after the daughter (aged 14) had disclosed sexual abuse. In keeping with the maxim that role-play clients are often more difficult than 'real' clients, the daughter was sullen, unco-operative, and made it clear that she did not want to be present.

In response to my early questions, the exact nature of the present difficulties was unclear. Mum variously said that she was concerned that she and Julie were not getting on since 'this had all come out', that she was worried about the effects of the abuse on Julie, and that Julie had been having outbursts of rage. Julie stated that she could not imagine any way in which things could be better, and protested that her Mum didn't have a clue what it was like for her.

After trying to elicit exceptions without much success, I asked them both 'Let's pretend for a minute that we could make a miracle happen, and tonight while you were asleep this miracle took place, and tomorrow morning you woke up and things were better. How would you know? What would be different?'

Julie: *How would I know that they were better?*

Kate: *Yeah, how would you know this miracle took place? What would be different? How would things be better?*

Julie: *At home?*

Kate: *Yeah ... or, in your life.*

Julie: *I'd have breakfast cooked for me.*

Kate: *Okay, what else? (pause) Has breakfast ever been cooked for you?*

Mum: *All the time!*

Julie: *But not with what I want!*

Kate: *Which would be what?*

Julie: *Pancakes.*

Kate: *Okay, so what else would be different?*

Mum: *And chocolate milkshakes!*

Kate: *Chocolate milkshakes?!*

Julie: *That's all.*

Kate: *Okay, you'd know that this miracle took place because you'd have pancakes for breakfast.*

Julie: *With maple syrup.*

Kate: *Okay ... would anything else be different? Would you be different in any way? Would Mum be different? Would Mark (younger brother) be different?*

Julie: *Mum would be different because she'd be pleased to make me pancakes.*

Kate: *Okay, so she'd be happily making pancakes.*

Julie: *Yeah!*

Kate: *And how would that make a difference?*

Julie: *Well, I'd feel like she wanted to please me.*

Kate: *Okay, so you'd feel like mum wanted to please you. And how would that make things better for you?*

Julie: *I'd just feel like, oh I don't know. (pause) Well, if you want to please somebody, then it must mean that you care about them.*

Kate: *So, does that mean that mum making pancakes and wanting to please you, that would be a sign to you, that would let you know that mum cared about you?*

Julie: *Um hum.*

Kate: *I don't want to put words in your mouth. Is that what you were saying?*

Julie: (nods head)

Kate: *And is that important to you? To know that mum cares about you?*

Julie: (pauses) *Well, I suppose so.*

Kate: *Yeah, that's something that's good to know?*

Julie: *Yeah.*

Kate: (to Mum) *And what about for you? What would this, how would you know this miracle took place?*

Mum: (laughs) *I'll make a thousand pancakes!*

Kate: (laughs) *Okay!*

Mum: *Yeah, that she didn't throw whatever I made back at me.*

Kate: *And what would she do instead?*

Mum: *She'd give me a peck on the cheek or something.* (pause) *Like she used to.*

Kate: *Like she used to. Okay, and how will that make a difference for you?*

Mum: *That she's responding to what I'm giving her.*

Kate: *Okay. And what would that tell you about Julie, or about you, or about your relationship, her responding?*

Mum: *That she cares.*

It was important that I persist with clarifying the nature of the solution-state and not launch into exception questions such as: 'So, when was the last time your Mum cooked pancakes for you?'

This interchange had allowed both Mum and Julie to begin to think about a future time when things would be different and to rehearse in their minds some of the features of that time. It also clarified for me the nature of their concerns. What was most salient for them both was the effects of the abuse on their mother-daughter relationship. This led to my being able to ask about exceptions with the question: 'So, what have you noticed about the way your Mum goes about showing you that she cares about you?' a question that invited concrete examples of times the desired state was already occurring. With a similar question to Mum, the session proceeded with discussion of times they got on better, didn't hassle each other, gave each other appropriate *space, and so on, and both reported that they were feeling much more hopeful by the end of the session.*

In relation to self-perception, future oriented questions may be posed to invite the client to consider the implications of the emerging new view of self. The self-perception questions outlined above allow the client to begin to identify and describe a way of thinking about self that differs from the old, abuse-dominated way. Making these ideas about self explicit seems to afford them greater impact. Questions about their implications follow naturally:

- *So, let's say you are able to think about yourself in that way over the next week, what difference do you suppose it will make?*
- *You said that these couple of things you've done to not let the feelings run your life tell you that you can be your own person. Now that you know that, how might things be different? Do you think you'll do some things in the next couple of weeks that you wouldn't have been able to do before you knew this?*

CASE EXAMPLE 6 - Michael Durrant

Angela, a 42 year old woman, had been sexually assaulted by her father in her early teens. In her attempts to avoid being alone with him, she refused to accompany him to the swimming pool one day, where he subsequently had a fall and drowned. She had carried her guilt about the abuse and about his death for many years. Recently, she felt she was a failure as a wife and mother, was unable to control her adolescent daughter, and was suffering panic attacks (the reason for the referral). She told me of the many ways that guilt had dominated her life and the ways she had tried to atone for her shortcomings by sacrificing herself for her mother, her husband and her children. She never disagreed with anyone, never stood up for herself, and was terrified in social situations that she would embarrass her family and friends.

Questions about the fact that she successfully maintained a responsible job elicited little, since she saw her 'coping' at work as being something she just had to do, and I quickly realised that it would be unhelpful to try to 'convince' Angela that this represented an exception. However, in the second session, Angela commented that she had seen a counsellor previously but had stopped going because her mother thought it a waste of time. She said that she had told her mother, a few days previously, that she was now attending therapy again and had not been surprised at her mother's response that this was unnecessary and stupid. I expressed some surprise that Angela had kept this appointment, since it seemed she was going against her mother's view. There was a lengthy discussion about Angela's reactions to her mother's comments, the thoughts that had led to her even volunteering the information to her mother, and her struggle in deciding to continue with therapy anyway. Questions about how she had managed this step brought comments such as 'I decided it was time to do something that I thought I needed', and my questioning about what this told Angela about herself led to her commenting 'I guess maybe I'm stronger than I thought I was'.

As this exception and the new self-perception that it suggested were explored and enlarged upon, Angela began to 'remember' other exceptions - times when she had stood up for herself in some small way or had believed in her own position. These were all small and tentative.

The second half of the session was devoted to speculation about what this emerging information about her strength might mean for the future. I asked questions such as: 'So does it surprise you to discover that you have more strength than you thought?' 'Is this a new idea about yourself?' 'How do you think you are able even to begin to think that way about yourself in the face of the guilt that has been taking over your life?' As Angela's statements about her own strength became slightly stronger, I wondered about the implications of this view: 'So, say you are able to continue to know that you have more strength than you thought, how do you think the next few days will be different?' Angela described in detail how she would manage her daughter more firmly, without being immobilised by fears that her daughter would reject her. 'Do you think you are ready to keep entertaining these new ideas about yourself as being strong, or do you think the feelings will try to bury the ideas?' When she maintained that she was ready to continue with these ideas: 'So, what is it about yourself that tells you that you are ready to keep on with these new ideas?'

As these questions, and more specific questions about how the next week would be different, continued, Angela was able to imagine and describe herself being stronger in a variety of situations, and I encouraged her to describe in detail the things she would be doing that would let her know she was following the ideas. She left the session obviously confident in her newfound *abilities (even though some of them had not yet happened) and returned having achieved a number of the things she had imagined.*

TALKING ABOUT TALKING ABOUT THE ABUSE

Among the principles of therapy with the effects of sexual abuse that we have suggested is: 'It is not necessary to discuss details of the abuse directly in order to diminish the effects. Clients are the best judges of whether, and when, it is helpful to discuss the abuse explicitly'.

Many approaches to therapy with clients who have been sexually abused include an expectation, or overt prescription, that the client will 'tell her story' of the abuse. It is variously argued that recounting the details in a trusting and supportive environment allows clients to come to terms with what happened, that this allows clients to vent their anger and other feelings which must be expressed in order for healing to occur, that such discussion provokes a cathartic crisis, and so on.

Our concern is that clients who experienced abuse as a violent, intrusive, or distressing experience may experience being asked to 're-live' the events as similarly violent, intrusive and distressing. As such, the prescription that clients must recount the details strikes us as oppressive and abusive.

Moreover, such a process may actually work against the process of developing a self-perception based on notions of competence. We have suggested that the feelings and experiences associated with the abuse effect the overall context within which the person begins to make sense of self, and that the continued interpreting of behaviour and emotion in terms of this context allows an abuse-dominated view of self to develop and strengthen. It follows that a prescribed recounting of the abuse itself may be associated with the same feelings and experiences and so may serve to further strengthen this view of self.

Our view is that clients, even children, are able to decide whether, and when, it is helpful for them to talk about the details of the abuse. It is not uncommon to find clients who say: 'I'm so sick of talking about it. I have had to talk to the police, the doctors and the welfare, and I don't feel like talking about it again'; or who say: 'It is too painful to talk about, and I don't want to do that'; or who talk a little about what happened but then decide they do not wish to pursue this. We might make sense of such statements as evidence of denial or of inability to come to terms with what happened, or we might make sense of them in terms of the client being in a position to know what is helpful.

Even if we do not overtly prescribe that clients must recount the details, it must be recognised that many clients come to therapy with the expectation that they will be required to do so. We find it helpful to be open about the issue of whether or not to talk about it:

- *Some people I see find it helpful to talk a bit about what actually happened to them and this seems to help them feel they can leave it behind. Some others feel that they can move forward without talking about the details. I'll need you to let me know what you think might be best for you.*

- *How do you think you'll know whether or not you'll want to talk more about what actually happened? I guess, from what you've said, that maybe you've got used to feeling like you can't make decisions, so how do you think you were able to decide that not talking about it today was what you wanted?*

- *I can understand what you mean when you say that you didn't plan to talk about the abuse at all today, and it will be up to you how much you talk about it next time. Did it surprise you that you were able to talk about it a bit today? What difference do you think that will make for you?*

In this way, the issue of 'to talk about it or not to talk about it' can itself provide opportunities for highlighting aspects of clients' competence and their knowledge of what is best for them. In a sense, these are themselves exceptions, since clients who have been sexually abused have often become well-practised in thinking that they are unable to make decisions, especially treatment decisions, for themselves. It is this process of utilising the process of therapy to encourage a view of competence and mastery that is more important than whether or not the abuse itself is ever talked about.

We should stress that we acknowledge that experiences of abuse, as with other trauma, may precipitate often profound and often confusing emotional reactions in children and adults. Moreover, we do not wish to assert that such children and adults may not be helped by the experience of talking about what happened to them in a supportive environment. However, we believe that the **demand**, explicit or otherwise, that clients recount the details and their feelings about them is itself abusive. Porter, Blick & Sgroi (1982) assert that:

... helping the child to focus on the abuse in a healthy perspective begins to relieve their emotional burden. (p.130)

As outlined above, our experience suggests that this may be the case, but equally that 'helping' such a focus on the abuse may add to the emotional burden. Sometimes our therapy will include a focus on the abuse itself, other times the client will choose to discuss the facts of the abuse with someone outside the therapy situation, and still other times the abuse is never discussed explicitly. Our overriding principle is that the client is the best judge of this decision, although the therapist has the task of establishing the therapeutic context within which the client can experience, and exercise, the ability to make such a judgement.

This, of course, begs the question of whether effective therapy can be done without the abuse experience ever being discussed. Not only do we believe this to be the case, but we also suggest that many therapists have seen clients who have been sexually abused in the past but who have never mentioned this occurrence, yet effective therapy may well have happened.

It is our focus on the effects of abuse, rather than on the abuse itself, and on a solution-focus, rather than a problem-focus, that leads to this conclusion. A problem-focus requires that the problem be identified and resolved, and effective therapy is impossible without this. A solution-focus implies that it is the embracing of solutions and the achievement of a solution state that are important, and that the experience of this has significant and profound effects on the way a client sees his or her future and the capabilities available to him or herself. We have suggested as a central tenet of our approach that an effect of abuse is to promote an abuse-dominated view of self, which determines the interpretation of events and emotion in such a way as to perpetuate any difficulties which may have been triggered by it ('the effects of abuse'). The corollary of this is that the building of a competent view of self may lead to a client being able to overcome the effects and envisage a life without them. A new view of self as competent may mean that the abuse, while still existing in memory, is no longer a pertinent factor in the client's way of making sense of her ongoing experience and so addressing it explicitly may be irrelevant.

The idea that the solution may not necessarily appear related to the presenting problem or complaint (de Shazer 1985), encourages us to pursue what clients find helpful. White's (1989) idea that the discovery of exceptions or unique outcomes and the 'performance of meaning' around these events leads to clients evolving a new story of themselves, which entails a 're-writing of their history', leads us to be confident that the pursuit of what clients find helpful, and the building of a new self-perception based on this, may lead to their re-writing the history of their abuse in such a way that it is no longer pertinent.

CASE EXAMPLE 7 - Michael Durrant

Stephen, aged 14 years, attended with his parents who were concerned that he had not resolved the trauma of his prolonged sexual assault by his older foster brother which had occurred for two years until the age of ten. They were concerned that he was unable to talk about his experiences, and had had two unsuccessful attempts at sexual abuse counselling, and that his distress was manifesting itself in a general lack of motivation, poor social skills, and stealing. They were particularly concerned about a single instance of Stephen sexually interfering with his younger brother, Andrew.

It was apparent to me that previous therapists had tried to encourage Stephen to talk about his experiences of abuse and that this had simply been 'more of the same' of what his parents had been doing - cajoling, pleading, and trying to manoeuvre him into talking. Realising that, even just to engage this young man, it would be important to do something different. I began by asking Stephen about how it was that he had stopped sexually abusing his younger brother. I added that many boys who had been sexually abused seemed to develop the idea that they couldn't control their own sexuality, since they had had some pretty powerful things happen to them that they couldn't control, but that it seemed that maybe Stephen had found some way to control his. (It has been apparent that Stephen had ceased his abusive behaviour prior to it being disclosed by his younger brother.) Stephen was unsure how he had done this, and initially explained it in terms of his brother having told him to stop and so on. I gently refused to accept this, since Stephen knew he was bigger and stronger than Andrew and could have forced himself upon him, and Stephen began to suggest that he just knew it was wrong.

Building on this exception as an example of self-control, I proceeded to ask Stephen about other times that he had shown himself that he was able to control his own urges. Much of the five or six sessions that followed were spent discussing times that Stephen could have stolen money but had resisted his urge to do so. A young man of low-to-average intelligence, Stephen was able to grasp that these events suggested he had the ability to control his urges and admitted to being surprised by this discovery. Together with me, and in some sessions with his parents, Stephen began to build a picture of himself as competent and in control of his life. His stealing ceased and he seemed to be getting along better with friends.

In a later session where his father was still concerned about whether Stephen had 'come to terms with his sexuality', I commented that I had not really spent much time discussing what had happened to Stephen and wondered if Stephen would think that helpful. Stephen replied, quite confidently: 'No, I have put that behind me. I know it happened, but I don't really think about it a lot. It's more important that I keep keeping out of trouble and catch up on my schoolwork.' Discussion of Stephen's new way of thinking about himself and the things he had learned about his ability to have some control in his life made it clear that he was moving forward and had, indeed, left his parents' concerns behind.

CONCLUSION

Much of our training encourages us to embrace the role of 'expert'. We are comfortable with the notion that we have expertise in ways of framing difficulties and asking questions that may encourage clients to begin to see themselves differently. On the other hand, we are uncomfortable with the notion that we know better than our clients what it is that they find helpful.

A problem of abuse-focused approach to therapy has the inherent risk of encouraging a process that we believe does not enhance clients' experience of themselves as competent and able to move forward. A solution-focus has allowed us to work co-operatively with our clients (while still being clear that we take the lead in many ways) to build upon those things they are doing that are pertinent to them and are contradictions to the abuse-dominated view they have developed of themselves.

Our therapy with clients who have experienced sexual abuse may be long or may not be, and it is often difficult. However, we find that a focus on assisting clients to use those existing examples of competence to develop new self-perceptions that may equip them to interact differently with the world, not only seems to fit for them, but also helps us not to become 'bogged down' in the enormity of the abusive experience. It is important to us that the complexity and magnitude of those experiences that have immobilised them should not immobilise us.

NOTES

1. A similar concern might be expressed about people continuing to define themselves as 'alcoholic', even many years after they stop drinking. Such a problem-centred description serves to keep the problem alive as part of the person's view of self; thus the person can never really feel that he or she has overcome the problem. That is, there remains in the individual's view of self a significant deficit or failing, which must impede the experience of competence or achievement.

2. A similar move from observation to prescription may be seen to have occurred in the area of grief counselling, where therapists have observed clients having particular experiences, which therapists choose to describe in terms of stages, and which then become prescriptions of how clients will experience their emotions and reactions - leading to referrals of clients who are 'not grieving properly' (that is, not grieving according to the therapist's schema of how one should grieve).

ACKNOWLEDGEMENTS

We wish to express our thanks to: Brian Cade, Eve Lipchik and Jane Durrant for their comments on an earlier draft of this chapter.

REFERENCES

Bateson, G. 1980:
    Mind and Nature: A necessary unity. New York, Bantam.
Berger, P. & Luckmann, T. 1966:
    The Social Construction of Reality. New York, Doubleday.
Davis, M. 1986:
    'Brief therapy: focused solution development.'Family Process, 25(2):207-222.
de Shazer, S. 1985:
    Keys to Solutions in Brief Therapy. New York, W.W.Norton.
de Shazer, S. 1988:
    Clues: Investigating solutions in brief therapy. New York, W.W.Norton.
de Shazer, S., Berg, I.K., Lipchik, E., Nunnally, E., Molnar, A., Gingerich, W. & Weiner-Dolan, Y. 1989:
    'Only once if I really mean it: brief treatment of a previously dissociated incest case.'
    Journal of Strategic & Systemic Therapies, 8(4):3-8.
Durrant, M. 1987:
    'Therapy with young people who have been victims of sexual assault.' Family Therapy Case Studies, 2(1):57-63.

Durrant, M. 1989:
'Temper taming: an approach to behaviour problems of children - revisited.' **Dulwich Centre Newsletter**, Autumn.

Epston, D. 1984:
'Guest address - Fourth Australian Family Therapy Conference.'**Australian Journal of Family Therapy**, 5(1):11-16.

Erickson, M.H., Rossi, E. & Rossi, S. 1976:
Hypnotic Realities. New York, Irvington.

Kelly, G. 1963:
A Theory of Personality. New York, W.W.Norton.

Kowalski, K. 1987:
'Overcoming the impact of sexual abuse: a mother's story.'**Family Therapy Case Studies**, 2(2):13-18.

Lipchik, E. 1988:
'Purposeful sequences for beginning the solution-focused interview.' In Lipchik, E. (Ed.) **Interviewing**. Rockville, Mass., Aspen.

Lipchik, E. & de Shazer, S. 1986:
'The purposeful interview.' **Journal of Strategic & Systemic Therapies**, 5(1): 88-99.

Little, W., Fowler, H.W. & Coulson, J. 1973:
The Shorter Oxford English Dictionary. Oxford, Clarendon Press.

O'Hanlon, W. & Weiner-Davis, M. 1989:
In Search of Solutions: A new direction in psychotherapy. New York, W.W.Norton.

Penn, P. 1985:
'Feed-forward: future questions, future maps.'**Family Process**, 24:299-311.

Porter, F.S., Blick, L.C. & Sgroi, S.M. 1982:
'Treatment of the sexually abused child.' In Sgroi, S. (Ed.) **Handbook of Clinical Intervention in Child Sexual Abuse**. Lexington, Mass., Lexington Books.

Sgroi, S.M. 1982:
'An approach to case management.' In Sgroi, S. (Ed.) **Handbook of Clinical Intervention in Child Sexual Abuse**. Lexington, Mass., Lexington Books.

Tomm, K. 1987:
'Interventive interviewing.'**Family Process**, 26:167-183.

Tomm, K. 1989:
'Externalizing problems and internalizing personal agency.'**Journal of Strategic & Systemic Therapies**.

Trepper, T.S. & Barrett, M.J. 1989:
Systemic Treatment of Incest. New York, Brunner/Mazel.Watzlawick,P.,

Weakland, J. & Fisch, R. 1974:
Change: Principles of problem formation and problem resolution. New York, W.W.Norton.

Weakland, J., Fisch, R., Watzlawick, P. & Bodin, A. 1974:
'Brief therapy: focused problem resolution.' **Family Process**, 13(2):141-168.

White, M. 1984:
'Pseudo-encopresis: from avalanche to victory, from vicious to virtuous cycles.' **Family Systems Medicine**, 2(2):150-160.

White, M. 1988:
'The process of questioning: a therapy of literary merit?' **Dulwich Centre Newsletter**, Winter.

White, M. 1988/89:
'The externalizing of the problem.' **Dulwich Centre Newsletter**, Summer.

White, M. & Epston, D. 1989:
Literate Means to Therapeutic Ends. Adelaide, Dulwich Centre Publications. (republished in 1990 as **Narrative Means to Therapeutic Ends**. New York, W.W.Norton.)

CHAPTER IV

HOSTILITY, APATHY, SILENCE & DENIAL:

Inviting abusive adolescents
to
argue for change

by

Richard Elms

Adolescents who have been emotionally, physically or sexually abusive, and people associated with them, describe a variety of characteristics of the adolescents and their relationships. They may have difficulty with responsibility and/or problems with dependency (conversely, their parents may be super-responsible or super-dependable); they may deny they have been abusive or may blame others for their actions; they may be easily influenced by their peers; they may have a pre-occupation with their own ideas and feelings, and difficulty in considering those of others; they often have poor social skills (for example, relating to younger children, using force or threats to get what they want); they may experience feelings of righteousness, rage, incompetence, helplessness, hopelessness, shame, guilt, worthlessness, etc. Many adolescents who have been abusive report fear of the legal consequences of their behaviour, fear of losing relationships, and fear of themselves and what they could do. Most adolescents who have been abusive seem reluctant to attend therapy, and many are downright hostile.

These kinds of circumstances and characteristics make the task of engaging abusive adolescents in therapy particularly challenging. This chapter describes some of the ideas and practises I have found helpful in addressing this challenge. The work of Michael White (e.g. 1986, 1989) in general, and of Alan Jenkins (e.g. 1990) with abusive men and adolescent sexual assault perpetrators, has been particularly influential and inspirational.

AIMS OF THERAPY

My aims in working with adolescents who have abused include (following Jenkins 1990):
- facilitate 'facing up' to problems - including acknowledging the nature and extent of abuse, facing the legal consequences, and facing any embarrassment, shame, guilt or fear associated with the process;
- promote the taking of responsibility by these adolescents for their abusive behaviour and their lives generally;
- facilitate an understanding of why the abuse occurred;

- facilitate an understanding of the potential impact of abuse on the victims;
- promote the development of more caring and respectful relationships.[1]

ASSUMPTIONS UNDERLYING THE APPROACH

To achieve the aims of therapy I find it helpful to understand the beliefs or perspectives through which abusive adolescents (and their families) make sense of themselves, their relationships and the abuse. Such beliefs or perspectives are seen as determinants of people's behaviour and patterns of interaction, and as potential obstacles (or restraints)[2] to 'facing up', 'taking responsibility', and the development of alternative styles of relating.

It is my assumption that our beliefs, feelings, behaviour and relationships interact and influence each other, and that they are influenced by social values, the values and practises of our families and others important to us, and by various other experiences. Abusive behaviour, then, is understood in terms of the interaction of these kinds of factors. I also assume that the characteristics of abusive adolescents described above are not an intrinsic part of their make-up or their relationships, and do not have to be permanent features. The approach outlined in this chapter, therefore, seeks to incorporate consideration of the broad context within which abuse occurs.[3]

Since most perpetrators of abuse will continue to be involved in relationships (e.g. with their own families, other families and individuals), working with them can be seen to have a preventative function.

A THERAPY OF QUESTIONS

The process of therapy in which I engage is primarily one of questioning. Several authors have influenced this particular style. For example, White (1988, p.9) has described a process of 'relative influence' questioning in which people are invited to describe, on the one hand, the influence of problems in their lives and relationships and, on the other hand, the influence of their lives and relationships in the life of the problem. He has noted (1988, 1989) that this process has people puzzling over contradictions, confronted with gaps in their knowledge of self, others and relationships, and that it encourages the filling of these gaps.

Epston & White (1989) have described an approach in which such contradictions and gaps are understood in terms of the 'storying' of experience, that is, people experience problems when the narratives or stories with which they (and/or others) make sense of themselves, their lives and relationships, do not sufficiently represent their lived experience. In these circumstances there will be significant aspects of their lived experience which contradict these dominant stories.

The focus of therapy becomes the identification and/or generation of alternative stories which bring with them new possibilities. Epston & White suggest that those aspects of lived experience which fall outside the dominant stories provide fertile ground for the generation of alternative stories. They have referred to such aspects as 'unique outcomes' and have described a process of questioning which facilitates their identification and use in the construction of alternative stories and possibilities.

In his work with abusive men (1990) and adolescent perpetrators of sexual assault (1987), Jenkins has described a process of therapy, utilising questioning, which assists perpetrators to face up to their abuse, take full responsibility for it, understand the impact of abuse on the victims, and to develop more respectful relationships.

Rather than emphasizing the classification of problems, or promoting the therapist as knowledgeable and expert (in the sense of providing answers or instructions), such a process of questioning emphasizes people's experience of events, their own knowledge, and expertise. It also promotes people's active participation in the generation of alternative perspectives and solutions, rather than the therapist diagnosing and prescribing or advising. Such approaches facilitate people thinking for themselves, and assist them to draw upon and develop their own resources, rather than depending on the ideas and resources of the therapist.[4] Thus, a therapy grounded in such a form of questioning seeks to establish a therapeutic process which promotes responsibility and independence - issues usually of particular significance in the case of adolescents who have been abusive.

Of course, the way in which questions are asked has a significant bearing on their effectiveness. For example, clients may feel interrogated, overwhelmed, incompetent or inadequate if they do not understand or cannot answer the questions.[5] They may also feel 'techniqued'. The potential for such problems can be minimised by a style incorporating respect, empathy, gentleness, sensitivity, curiosity, co-operation, the use of vocabulary and concepts that are understandable to the people involved, and by proceeding at a pace that is suitable for them.

THE THERAPIST-ADOLESCENT RELATIONSHIP

I have found that engaging abusive adolescents in therapy is facilitated by a climate in which the therapist conveys concern and support, not only for the victims of abuse, but for the perpetrator as well. Establishing such a climate provides a helpful framework within which to oppose abuse and its effects, and does not have to lead to any conflict of interest with victims.[6] Rather, establishing this climate assists the therapist to help the adolescent face difficult issues. It also assists the therapist to recognise, support and respect efforts the adolescent makes to deal with such issues.

While distress, anger and the like are entirely appropriate responses for a therapist to have towards abuse, I believe that the manner in which they are expressed, and their effect on one's work, are important subjects for critical review. My own experience has been, for example, that if I am feeling infuriated during an interview my thinking can easily become clouded, and I am more likely to do or say something unhelpful. Developing patience and the ability to identify 'unique outcomes', being prepared to proceed a step at a time at the adolescent's pace, and realising that setbacks or backward steps are often associated with the process of change, can be of assistance in such situations. It may also be helpful at some stage to invite the adolescent to explore and develop an understanding of the therapist's and others' thoughts and feelings about the abuse.

SAFETY AND WELLBEING OF VICTIMS

In this approach, emphasis is placed on the needs of the victims of abuse. I believe it is consistent with the aims of therapy for perpetrators of abuse to take whatever steps are necessary to contribute to the safety and wellbeing of victims. Before initial interviews, enquiries would be made with the referring person, state welfare authorities, etc., about the steps that had been taken to protect and support the victim. These measures are reviewed with these people, with the adolescent perpetrator, and with caregivers on an ongoing basis. In many cases (especially those involving sexual or extreme physical abuse) it is appropriate for such steps to include a period of separation of the adolescent from victims and/or potential victims. Separation can be both a safety measure and a means of providing 'space' for the victims to work on overcoming the effects of the abuse. It can be an opportunity for the adolescent to begin (or extend) the revision of his/her life and relationships. If an adolescent agreed to separate for these reasons, it would be an example of 'facing up' and 'taking responsibility'.[7]

Some of my work with abusive adolescents has begun when they were referred to residential care programmes - a situation in which they can feel abandoned, hopeless and vulnerable to giving up on themselves and the hope of improved relationships. It is particularly important, then, for such separations to be promoted as a positive step for the victims of abuse and as an opportunity for the adolescents themselves. Ideally, of course, the residential programme should be one which can assist the adolescents in the ongoing revision of their life and relationships as they 'face up' and 'take responsibility'.

Other examples of ensuring that victims are safe and have 'space' would be: suspension or expulsion from school; the adolescent perpetrator ensuring he/she remains under adult supervision at school, home, or at other times he/she has contact with potential victims. Resuming contact with victims would only occur when the victims were ready for it, and when plans for ensuring their ongoing safety were in place. Emphasis would be placed on parents, the perpetrator and others focussing primarily on the needs of the victim(s). The whole process of evaluating the perpetrator's progress depends upon corroboration of reported changes by people associated with him or her - family, victim(s) (and/or their counsellors), teachers, youthworkers, fellow residents if in a residential programme, etc.

THE PROCESS OF THERAPY

In the first interview, I begin the process of obtaining, from the abusive adolescent and/or others who are present, information about the nature and extent of abuse, and about the adolescent's life and relationships generally. I try to be aware of opportunities to explore links between people's beliefs (and behaviour) and other experiences or influences, including social values (such as those related to gender roles and parenting), peer pressure, family values and practises, and so on. Exploring these links can contribute significantly to the generation of alternative or broader perspectives (and therefore to the possibility of new solutions), and can assist people to comprehend what may have been incomprehensible to them. Exploring these links is an ongoing part of therapy as people frequently become more aware of, or more comfortable with sharing about, experiences which have influenced them - for example, they may disclose having been abused themselves.

A major assumption is that people are in relationship with ideas, feelings, patterns of interaction and ways of behaving, social values, family 'traditions', etc.[8] They may be 'embracing' them, 'co-operating' with them, 'dominated' or 'influenced' by them, 'tricked', 'sucked-in' or 'conned' by them. I have found it helpful to enquire about the adolescent's (and family's) thoughts and feelings about the abuse, its effects, events since the abuse was discovered, and about any other problems he/she may have. I have then found it particularly helpful to enquire about the kind of lifestyle and relationships he/she would prefer to have (however, I don't count on the adolescent co-operating with these enquiries). During this stage of therapy the adolescent may be invited to 'question', 'defy', 'depart from', 'escape from', 'disrespect', 'stand up to', 'rebel against' or 'disobey' those influences which have contributed to the abuse.[9] This whole process sets a context, and establishes 'themes' which form the basis of ongoing therapy.

The direction of these enquiries relates to the reported experiences of the adolescent, his/her family, the therapist, and others, rather than to assumptions about 'characteristics' of abusive adolescents and their relationships. Such assumptions, if mistaken, increase the difficulty of engaging the adolescent and his/her caregivers in therapy. The process of engagement is facilitated by the use of vocabulary and concepts that are meaningful to the adolescent and his/her family. Ideally, I will employ vocabulary and concepts derived from the language used by the adolescent and family, rather than imposing my own. An exception to this principle would be when adolescents and/or their caregivers use language which minimises the seriousness and effects of their actions. For example, I would substitute words like 'assault' and 'abuse' for 'looking after himself' (i.e.

beating up other people), 'playing with' or 'interfering with' (sexually). I would also refrain from using abusive or offensive language.

HOSTILITY, APATHY, SILENCE & DENIAL

Most people who have worked with adolescents will be familiar with responses like 'dunno' and 'don't care', and may have experienced frustration when they have tried to convince or persuade them of anything. Some adolescents say very little, and some nothing at all. Sometimes this seems to be related to hostility, and sometimes to the difficulty associated with facing and talking about problems. Some adolescents just seem to find it very difficult to think and speak for themselves.

Jenkins (1990, 1987) has described questions which constitute 'irresistible invitations to responsibility' for sexual offenders. I have found these kinds of questions helpful in working with abusive adolescents generally, and especially those who present as hostile or uncommunicative. These questions usually invite the adolescent to make a statement about the preferred direction of his/her life and relationships, and are often addressed to parents or other caregivers if the adolescent is not answering questions:

- *Do you think he is training for a career as a child abuser?*
- *Would you prefer to relate to little kids for the rest of your life - or would you like to learn how to relate to people your own age?*
- *Are you content to relate to pictures in magazines - or would you like to learn to get on with real people in respectful ways? (Where pornography has been an influence.)*
- *Do you think he wants to continue practising to be a bully - or do you think he wants to be the sort of person who considers other's feelings?*
- *Do you want to be the kind of person who thinks only of himself, and takes advantage of kids - or do you want to be the kind of person who cares for and protects them?*
- *Do you want to be a person who stands on their own feet and faces their own problems - or would you rather leave your problems for others to deal with (e.g. parents, victims)?*

When adolescents say they do wish to change, it can be helpful for the therapist to be cautious about whether or not they have made an informed decision - at least until the implications of change have been explored further:

- *Facing a problem like this, and really understanding the effects of your abuse on other people, could be a very hard thing to do. Don't you think it could be a lot less distressing for you to cop out and leave it all up to your parents/victim/s to deal with?*

- *Are you sure you know what you could be up against though? Lots of guys think that to be a real man you've got to act tough - be quick with your fists - you know - don't think about other people's needs and feelings - just think about yourself - and if others aren't big enough or tough enough - too bad. Do you know guys like that?*[10]

- *If you decided to break away, what would your friends say and do?*

- *Could you handle that? How? What plans can you make?*

Commenting and questioning in this way further contributes to a context in which it is the adolescent who argues for change.

Some adolescents deny they have been abusive at all. In these circumstances it can be helpful to ask 'hypothetical' questions of them and/or of their caregivers:

- *If a person had done something like this, what would it be like for them trying to decide whether or not to own up? What would they be thinking and feeling?*

- *Would it be easy, or would it take courage and strength to own up to something like this?*

- *Do you reckon a mature person would hide their problems and leave them for others to deal with - or would they own up to them and get whatever help is necessary?*

Another option is to enquire about the adolescent's reputation:

- *Does it concern you that people think you are abusive?*

- *What concerns you about that?*

- *What is it like not being trusted? How would you prefer people to think of you?*

The aim in each case is not to trick or force an admission from the adolescent. It is not even for the adolescent to answer any questions. Rather, the aim is to promote a climate in which the adolescent may feel a little more understood, and where issues related to abuse are considered from alternate perspectives (that is, in terms of responsibility and maturity).

The identification, acknowledgement, and attribution of meaning to occasions when the adolescent has 'owned up', faced problems, demonstrated responsibility, been strong, courageous or trustworthy, etc., is an important part of this process since it may assist him/her to recognise his/her capacity to 'face up' and to develop greater responsibility.[11]

Invariably there will be the occasional adolescents who, despite the therapist's best efforts to ask helpful questions, will say they don't care how people view them, or that they don't want to be mature, or that they think it is fun to abuse others, that they want to cultivate a reputation as someone to be scared of, etc. In these circumstances it can also be helpful to identify occasions they have not practised such a lifestyle, and to enquire further about this. Of course, it is important to avoid giving the impression that you are being sarcastic, or trying to be clever or 'smart':

- *You seem to be angry/upset at the moment - could you cope if I ask you some more questions which you might find difficult?*
- *Are you sure? I wouldn't want anger to get the better of you. Given what you have said, how come there have been a few times in our talk when you haven't shouted?*
- *How do you explain the few reports of kindness/responsibility that your parents/youth workers have told me about?*
- *Are you disappointed that these events don't fit with the abusive kind of life you said you want to practice?*
- *How come you're not as far into an abusive lifestyle as you could be?*
- *What would you have to do to make sure you got kindness and responsibility right out of your life?*

Whether the adolescent answers any of these questions or not, subsequent meetings can focus on whether or not there have been further instances of kindness, responsibility, etc., or instances where the adolescent was not as abusive as he/she could have been (for example, he/she may have sworn where previously he/she would have hit). The adolescent can then be asked to account for these developments. Since many of them see themselves as incapable of changing, and many seem to be aware only of those thoughts, feelings, actions, etc., which fit with an abusive lifestyle, this process assists them to re-define themselves, helping them to become aware of new possibilities for their lives. The frequency of non-abusive and responsible behaviour may begin to increase in these circumstances, and often adolescents decide they would prefer to practice an alternative lifestyle after all.

Usually (as in therapy generally), these alternative definitions and possibilites are competing with strong and long-held beliefs, feelings and behaviour, and are therefore tentative at first. They are often forgotten or lost - particularly in response to crises, setbacks, or relapses. It is important, then, for therapists to be persistent. It can also be helpful, once the adolescent has said he/she wishes to change, to predict the likelihood of setbacks or relapses, to invite the adolescent to speculate about their possible impact (and/or for the therapist to comment on how other adolescents have experienced them), and to discuss possible strategies for dealing with them.[12]

Needless to say, it is important for therapists to be patient in working with abusive adolescents, and to be able to review and critique the focus of their work, the helpfulness of the questions they ask, and the therapeutic climate they promote. Developing skill in the area of 'irresistable invitations', for example, will probably reduce the likelihood that adolescents will persist with saying they 'don't care', or that they wish to pursue abusive lifestyles.

'UNIQUE' OR 'EXCEPTIONAL' EVENTS AND THEIR MEANING

As already indicated, there are invariably aspects of the adolescent perpetrators' lives and relationships which don't completely fit with an abusive and irresponsible lifestyle. There may be occasions on which they have acted more responsibly than they could have, they may have indicated some level of concern for other people, they may have a preference for, or intend to practice, non-abusive behaviour. Discovering, accounting for, and speculating about the implications of these and subsequent 'unique outcomes' or 'exceptions'[13] is a major focus of ongoing therapy.

Adolescents and their caregivers are frequently unaware of the presence or potential significance of events such as these - their 'restraints', or the 'stories' through which they interpret their experience, obscure them. It is, therefore, important for therapists using this approach to develop their ability to identify, and to assist people to identify, 'unique' or 'exceptional' events, to assist them to attribute meaning and significance to them, and so help them develop new understandings and perspectives. Rather than being a process of 'pointing out positives' or of trying to persuade or convince, this is a process of 'invitational' questioning, with a flavour of exploration, curiosity and discovery.[14]

Often, apparently small or 'trivial' events (such as answering a few questions) seem to be the only 'unique' or 'exceptional' events available. However, under the circumstances for the person concerned, they can be quite significant. This implies a 'relative' rather than a 'normative' perspective by the therapist - that is, people are invited to measure their achievements or progress according to where they were up to before, or to where they could be if problems had more influence over them. This is in contrast to those measurements which relate to some standard of 'normality' or to the person's, therapist's, or other's hopes and expectations. While it can be helpful to have a goal, hopes, or a desired destination, a preoccupation with these and with how far one has to go to 'arrive', can be quite limiting. This form of measurement seems often to be associated with a sense of failure, or of not being 'up to standard', or of having an overwhelming distance still to go.[15] The relative form of measurement often seems to be associated with a sense of progress, enablement and empowerment:

- *Is this different for you?*
- *How would you have handled this situation before you had started to face up to your problems?*
- *How is he relating differently to his sister/brother now, compared to six months ago?*
- *How much worse could things be if you had allowed these feelings to take you over more?*
- *What difference could it make if you remembered some of the steps you have taken, instead of just the ones that lie before you?*
- *How do you understand the effects of your abuse on the victim/s now, compared to before?*

The following questions are examples of those that relate to the identification of 'unique outcomes', and to the process of attributing meaning or significance to them. They are categorised according to White's (1988) classification, and some address parents' or caregivers' side of the relationship. The language and concepts used in such questions derive from prior discussion about the adolescent's problems and their effects, and to 'themes' and links which have emerged, e.g. some questions would form part of the process of 'externalizing' social values.

Unique Outcome Questions:

- *Have there been any occasions that he has been more a brother than a bully?*
- *Has he made any attempts to practice responsibility since our last meeting?*
- *Have there been times recently when you could have been a sheep, and gone along with the crowd, but instead were your own person?*
- *Are you pleased you were able to rely on your own brains instead of other people's brains?*
- *Are you surprised he was able to stop himself from hitting him?*
- *Which of these events do you think I believe are examples of you pulling your own strings?[16]*
- *Have there been times you have risked facing him with opinions or situations he may find difficult?*
- *Are you surprised your parents didn't sort it out for you, but left you to rely on yourself?*
- *Was it hard for you to leave him to stand on his own two feet instead of making excuses for him?*

Unique Account Questions:

- *How were you able to defy the tradition for guys handed down in your family?*
- *What do your recent thoughts and decisions about not picking on your sister mean?*
- *Can you help me understand how you managed to rebel against what the group were saying?*
- *How were you (parents) able to make such a stand against violence?*
- *How were you able to stand up to the idea that you should do everything for the kids?*
- *What do you think this achievement tells me about new traditions you could be making for yourself?*
- *What does this step tell you about the nature of your new direction?*

Unique Redescription Questions:

- *What personal qualities could these achievements indicate?*
- *What could they indicate to me (and/or others)?*
- *What sides of you do you think are becoming more visible to others?*
- *What difference does realising this make to how you feel about, and treat, yourself?*
- *What aspects of your relationship are you appreciating more?*
- *What effect does knowing this about him have on your relationship with him?*

Unique Possibilities Questions:

- *What difference could these qualities make to your future?*
- *As you get better at defying the old traditions, what new traditions could you make for yourself?*
- *What do you think I believe is possible for you now, that wasn't possible for you before?*
- *How will your new future be different to the future of your old past?*

An important aspect of therapy with abusive adolescents is promoting alternative definitions of strength, maturity and (for boys) masculinity. Typically (and in keeping with values promoted by peers, in movies and magazines, etc., and often in their families), adolescents who have been abusive define strength, maturity and masculinity in terms of physical prowess, sexual experience, the capacity to control or dominate, and to be indifferent to the needs and feelings of others. With the exception of anger and 'lust', the expression of feelings is generally seen as weakness.

Alternative definitions of strength, maturity and masculinity usually include ideas about being able to face problems, to take responsibility, to think for oneself (rather than just going along with one's peers, family, social values, etc.), to face (and learn to express) emotions, to be able to understand others and put them before oneself, etc.

CASE EXAMPLE

Andrew, 14 years old, attended therapy with his mother, Jenny, and father, John. He had sexually assaulted his six year old sister on three occasions. The police had decided not to lay charges, and the State Welfare Department had said that Andrew could only remain in the home if he underwent counselling.

Jenny and John told me from the outset that they would oppose any attempt to separate the family as they believed it would be against everyone's interests. This opposition, they said, would including going to the 'highest court in the land' if necessary.

I explained that my main concern was the safety and wellbeing of their daughter and that, if they wanted, I also hoped to be able to assist them to ensure family relationships were happy, safe and satisfying for everyone. I said I would have to reserve judgement on whether or not separation could be a helpful part of this process until I had heard more about their situation.

Did Jenny and John think Andrew could cope with my asking him some questions about the abuse? They weren't really sure. 'What did Andrew think', I wondered. 'Could he handle me asking him some questions which he might find embarrassing, upsetting, or which he might get angry about?' He thought he could.

In a very quiet voice, with considerable hesitancy, and with the filling in of numerous gaps by his parents, Andrew was able to provide some details about the nature and extent of his abuse.

I then asked him how he explained his abuse of his sister. 'The guys at school talked about girls they had been with.' Did that mean he was easily influenced by others? He thought it did, and I asked if he could tell me a bit more about that. He never felt as good or as experienced as anyone else, he said, and he felt like the 'odd one out'. 'Did the guys at school talk about being with girls their own age or with girls much younger?' I asked. 'Their own age,' he muttered after quite a pause.

I enquired about the effects of the abuse on Andrew's parents. Jenny and John described their shock, their distress, and worries about the possible effects on their daughter, and losing trust in Andrew. Jenny talked about feelings of guilt - especially about her having returned to the workforce: 'If I was at home it might not have happened.' I wondered if she thought it was fair that a parent feel that they should always have to supervise a fourteen year old? No, she didn't. Did John think parents should have to control a teenager's behaviour for them? 'Well,' he suggested, 'there were still some things they had to learn, but they should certainly be able to be trusted with their sisters.' I asked Andrew if he thought it was more grown up or less grown up to be able to control and supervise yourself. 'More grown up', he thought. Did he think his abuse was someone else's fault? 'No.' Was he interested in facing up to his problems, then, or would he prefer to cop out? 'Face up.'

I asked if Jenny and John's statements meant they were resisting guilt, at least to some extent, and putting the blame where it belonged? They supposed they were, and Jenny went on to say that she was trying not to let it get on top of her - that they told themselves they had done their best, that things sometimes go wrong.

After discussing this further, I asked Andrew how he thought the abuse had affected his family. There was a long pause, during which Andrew became visibly more and more upset.[17] Finally, he started to cry, but managed to say through his sobs that: 'My mother cries ... I've been stupid ... I've made my mother sick.' Did he have any worries about effects on his sister? After he said 'Yes', I asked what sorts of worries, and he said he worried that she might not get over it.

John thought Andrew hadn't thought about the consequences of his actions, and that talking to him about problems was like 'water off a duck's back'. Were there other areas of his life in which he didn't think about the consequences of his actions? A substantial list followed, with the summary that Andrew was not as responsible as he should be for his age. I asked Andrew if he agreed with all of this - and he did. His parents went on to say that they felt they were continually 'on his back'. What was that like for Andrew? He said he didn't like it. Would he prefer to be on his own back? Definitely! We then discussed some ways that Andrew was acting in a more responsible, 'grown-up' way.

After this, I asked Andrew what sort of relationships he wanted with his family. He said he wanted his parents to be proud of him, and he wanted to be better than other people.[18] What if he couldn't be better than others - did he want to be able to handle this in a mature way? Yes, he wanted to use his abilities, and wanted the family to be close and happy. Did this mean he wanted to rebuild trust, to have relationships where everyone was safe and there was no fear of abuse, that he wanted to be more responsible and think of the consequences of his actions?, I asked. Andrew said he wanted each of *these.*

What kind of relationship did he want with his sister? 'To be a big brother.' 'What kind of big brother?' He didn't know. 'The kind of big brother who helps his sister with problems if she wants it, or the kind who gives his sister problems?' The first kind. Was he sure? 'Some people think it should be everyone for themselves - that you take what you can get.' He was sure. Did he want to be the kind of brother who respected his sister's needs and feelings, or the kind who pushes them aside? 'The first kind', he said. Was he interested in relating to girls his own age, or would he prefer to relate only to six year olds? His own age, he replied.

We then discussed steps that had been taken to ensure safety and 'space' for Andrew's sister. These included Andrew not being alone with her, keeping out of her bedroom, and ensuring that if she wanted to socialise with him it occurred around other people. I asked about the possibility that she may not understand these precautions, and perhaps think that there was something wrong with her, or that the abuse was her fault. Jenny and John had been stressing to her that the abuse was Andrew's fault, and were happy to continue doing so. They had made Andrew apologise and she had commenced counselling of her own.

We reviewed some ways that Andrew was already being the kind of brother he said he wanted to be, and some recent occasions he had (in his father's words) been 'his own man' instead of being a 'sheep' and going along with the crowd. I complimented Andrew on the capacity he had shown to answer some difficult questions and face some difficult issues. Inviting him, and his parents, to speculate about the meaning of those events, and on what difference they could make to the future of Andrew's life and relationships if he built on them, seemed to have the effect of introducing an element of hope - of new possibilities. This was in contrast to Andrew's apparent sense of despair and hopelessness - experiences which could well get in the way of change.

Jenny and John appeared to be less bewildered, less burdened by guilt, and to have a developing sense of resolve and direction. We concluded by agreeing to review the ongoing effectiveness of the safety and 'space' measures at future meetings. Andrew also asserted that he was ready to face up to his problems some more. I suggested that the path he had chosen would not necessarily be an easy one, and that it would take considerable courage for him to follow it. Jenny stated that if Andrew didn't 'pull his socks up' he might have to leave home after all - that his sister was the main priority now.

Subsequent meetings included clarifying further just what Andrew was thinking and feeling at the time of the abuse as a way of identifying any additional influences on him. During this enquiry Andrew admitted that he knew the abuse was wrong at the time, but pushed this knowledge aside (such an admission is an example of 'facing-up'). Andrew was also asked to provide more specific details about the abuse, and to describe how he had tricked his sister into participating. These lines of enquiry were intended to facilitate 'facing-up' and 'taking responsibility', as were questions (along the lines of Jenkins 1990, p.214) intended to help him understand the potential impact of his abuse.

I also pursued the themes of 'being his own man', becoming the kind of brother he wanted to be, 'using his abilities', learning to 'get on his own back' and developing a more 'mature' and responsible lifestyle. Later meetings were attended by Andrew's younger brother who also had 'problems with his growing up' and tended to pick on his sister. Andrew's sister also began to attend and participated in discussion about family relationships generally, as well as providing valuable perspectives on the nature of Andrew's relationship with her, his progress, and on areas that remained problematic. Her participation provided an opportunity to reinforce the idea of Andrew's responsibility for the abuse, and to address any other issues she wanted to raise.

The children's development of responsibility, generally, was facilitated by Jenny's resolve (with John's support) to depart from a tradition for the women on her side of the family. This tradition insisted that mothers should do everything for their families - from preparing all meals, cleaning the house, collecting and doing all their washing, making their beds, cleaning their rooms, etc., to providing transport whenever they wanted it. This tradition was not only exhausting (especially as Jenny had returned to the workforce - a departure from this tradition in itself), but also meant Jenny and John (also influenced by the idea that parents should be super-available to their children) had no time for themselves and their own relationship. Jenny and John's departures from this tradition (e.g. going out together for the first time in years, deciding that Andrew was old enough to remember for himself to study and do homework - and if he didn't he'd have to face the consequences), meant greater expectations of self-sufficiency on all the children - expectations with which they struggled and to which they progressively adjusted.

CONCLUSION

Working with adolescents, generally, and with those who have been abusive in particular, can be especially challenging. Many readers will be all too familiar with adolescents who respond with hostility, apathy, silence, or denial. Many will also be aware of the difficulty (perhaps futility) of trying to convince or persuade adolescents to change.

This chapter has focussed on various aspects of a general approach to working with adolescents who have been physically, sexually, or emotionally abusive. Abusive behaviour is considered within the context of social values, family values and experiences, peer group values and experiences, etc. Therapy seeks to address these influences and their effect on the adolescent's thinking, feelings, and behaviour.

The approach is one which seeks, primarily through a process of questioning, to facilitate the development of alternative perspectives of self, others, and relationships. It also seeks to promote the development of more respectful, caring relationships. Through the style of questioning employed, the therapist aims to contribute to a climate in which the adolescent, rather than the therapist, argues for change.

NOTES

1. I believe apologies made by perpetrators within the context of these aims will be more genuine and meaningful than those made solely on the basis of guilt or fear.

2. See Bateson (1972, p.399) for discussion of the idea of restraint, and White (1986) for an application of these ideas to therapy.

3. It is beyond the scope of this chapter to describe in detail some of the specific approaches that can be helpful in situations of abuse, e.g. Jenkins (1987) describes an approach to working with adolescent sexual assault perpetrators. He also provides a detailed description (1990) of the relationship between socio-cultural values and abuse.

4. Many people with this orientation to therapy have not, traditionally, been considered 'therapists' or 'experts'. For example, I know many youth workers who 'expertly' and 'therapeutically' assist young people to think for themselves, entertain different perspectives, be experts on themselves, and develop their own solutions.

5. Some confusion, uncertainty or disorientation is, however, often associated with questions which invite people to consider 'gaps' in their knowledge of events, themselves, others and their relationships (see White 1988, p.9). If people become apologetic or cannot answer, I often find it helpful to acknowledge that it is a difficult question, to say that they can take their time or that we can return to it later, and to compliment them on attempts to answer or to think about it.

6. I recognise, however, that some forms of concern and support may, even if unintentionally, leave unchallenged or actually support abusive actions, irresponsible lifestyles, and values which have influenced them. Making excuses for abusive behaviour, or protecting the perpetrator from the reasonable consequences of it, are examples.

7. See Menses & Durrant (1986) for a description of such a programme.

8. Michael White (1989) has referred to a process of 'separating' people from problems. He calls it 'externalizing' the problem, and has described 'relative influence' questioning as an 'externalizing practice'.

9. Many adolescents appear to be decidedly uncomfortable about the idea of 'co-operating', being 'dominated', 'tricked', 'sucked in' or 'conned'. The same adolescents usually find the idea of 'defying', 'escaping', 'disrespecting', 'rebelling', etc. to be much more appealing.

10. These particular examples of questions and comments are of the type that address cultural stereotypes about masculinity - stereotypes which may also fit with the adolescent's family's values and peer group values - and may be useful when working with adolescent boys. Thus they may be relevant and thought-provoking to other people who attend with the adolescent, e.g. parents, youth workers, etc.

11. See Jenkins (1990, p.124) for further ideas about responding to denial.

12. See White (1986, p.178) for discussion on 'relapses'.

13. de Shazer (1985) talks about 'exceptions' to the problem or 'complaint'.

14. Adolescents are notorious for their capacity to remain unconvinced by even the most persuasive reasoning. Attempting to persuade or convince in circumstances like these could also be seen as the therapist (or parents, etc.) doing all the work for change, or as thinking for the adolescent. The style of questioning used in this approach invites the adolescent to convince and persuade themselves.

15. Many readers will probably have had similar experiences in their thinking about their work and other parts of their lives.

16. This kind of question invites people to entertain the perspectives of others - perspectives which can be quite different to their own at that point in time, and which may well be conducive to change.

17. It can be tempting for therapists to move on to something else, or to help people out when pauses like this occur. However, in many circumstances, such pauses can provide an opportunity for people to face and struggle with difficult issues. They can also provide 'space' for adolescents to practice thinking and answering for themselves.

18. Adolescents who have been abusive often seem to feel inadequate, incompetent, etc. Feeling better about themselves is often associated with being bigger, stronger, tougher, smarter, better, and so on. For many this is most easily achieved by associating with (and often abusing) people who are smaller, weaker, less smart, etc.

REFERENCES

Bateson, G. 1972:
  Steps to an Ecology of Mind. New York, Ballantine Books.
de Shazer, S. 1985:
  Keys to Solutions in Brief Therapy. New York, W.W.Norton.
Epston, D. & White, M. 1989:
  Literate Means to Therapeutic Ends. Adelaide, Dulwich Centre Publications.
Jenkins, A. 1987:
  'Engaging the adolescent sexual abuser.' Unpublished workshop notes.
Jenkins, A. 1990:
  Invitations to Responsibility: The therapeutic engagement of men who are violent and abusive. Adelaide, Dulwich Centre Publications.
Menses, G. & Durrant, M. 1986:
  'Contextual residential care: the application of the principles of cybernetic therapy to the residential treatment of irresponsible adolescents and their families.' **Dulwich Centre Review** - also **Journal of Strategic & Systemic Therapies**, Summer.
White, M. 1986:
  'Negative explanation, restraint & double description: a template for family therapy.' **Family Process**, 25(2):169-184.
White, M. 1988:
  'The process of questioning: a therapy of literary merit?' **Dulwich Centre Newsletter**, Winter.
White, M. 1988/89:
  'The externalizing of the problem.' **Dulwich Centre Newsletter**, Summer.

CHAPTER V

SEXUAL ABUSE:

Two women's different ways of working
with the same problem
and
from the same perspective

by

Irene Esler
&
Jane Waldegrave

We begin with a description of our thinking in relation to the various contexts on which our work touches. This will allow the reader some idea of 'where we are coming from', our attitudes and values, assumptions and beliefs that influence our work.

In considering sexual abuse, we find ourselves thinking in relation to the following contexts:

- social, political and cultural context;
- the therapeutic context;
- the sexual abuse context.

MAIN PRINCIPLES THAT SERVE AS A BASE FOR THERAPEUTIC WORK

The therapist's thinking has a profound effect on his/her interactions with the people seen in therapy.

The therapist's own social, political and cultural analysis is inevitably incorporated into the therapeutic model of working the therapist uses.

ASSUMPTIONS ABOUT THE SOCIAL, POLITICAL & CULTURAL CONTEXT

We see the problem of sexual abuse as occurring within a social, political and cultural context. By this we mean that we view the abuse in a wider context than just the family context. Families are part of a wider system and the wider system influences families' beliefs. What happens in the family is a reflection of what happens in society.

We hold the view that we live in a society grounded in, and shaped by, patriarchal ideology, and our social, political and cultural analysis occurs within the context of this ideology. Society encourages patriarchal attitudes and actions. Society condones men having power over women and children. This encourages the subordinate status of women in society and in the family.

Culturally, a similar pattern occurs. The dominant culture has political, social and cultural power over minority cultures. Those who benefit most in our society are the white middle class (plus) males because society condones the domination of these cultural attitudes and actions. This encourages the subordinate status of minority cultures.

We see it as inevitable that families find themselves participating in abusive situations. Abusive situations are about one person having power over another person. Society creates an environment where men have power over women and families are victims of that.

ASSUMPTIONS ABOUT THE THERAPEUTIC CONTEXT
Our sexual, political and cultural analysis.

Since our analysis is set in the context of patriarchal ideology, our therapeutic model of working is greatly influenced by that analysis.

One of the implications for therapy of viewing abuse in a context wider than that of the family context, is that some of our questions centre around the influence of, and the connections between, patriarchal social attitudes and what happens in the family. We ask questions that attempt to deal with family members' beliefs and perceptions about themselves as a way of dealing with issues around patriarchy - questions such as: 'What would be your explanation for why so many people are silenced when they are in an abusive situation?'

Ideas about change.

A goal of therapy is to empower families to make changes so that things will be better for them. The family's stories need to be heard. They need to feel understood, validated and affirmed about their experience. It is then that they can contemplate change at the level of belief change.

New information brings about change. New information entails people thinking about their problems in a different way. Understanding the relationship patterns that occur among family members and how these are connected to the problem helps the therapist and the family to think about the problem in a different way.

Families have beliefs and assumptions about how things are. These ideas can restrain them or stop them from trying out different solutions to their problems. Our aim in therapy is to find ways to encourage the family to see things from a different perspective.

We adopt a curious and 'how come?' stance to avoid family members feeling blamed and judged. We also come from a position of respect, even if we don't like some of the things the family members have done.

The sorts of questions we ask are designed to:

• hear people's stories;
• understand the family's beliefs;
• understand family relationship patterns or interactional habits;
• understand the link between the problem and relationship patterns in the context of their beliefs;
• affirm people for the things they've done that show their good intentions;
• encourage people to observe from a 'meta level';
• encourage people to see their problem from a different viewpoint.

ASSUMPTIONS ABOUT SEXUAL ABUSE CONTEXT

Our attitudes and values affect how we work with families where sexual abuse has occurred. Our social, cultural and political analysis and our ideas about change give us a base from which to decide what we think about the abuser, victim and other family members and how we might work with them.

• We believe the abuser is responsible for the abuse. It is totally unacceptable behaviour and at no time do we want to appear to condone any part of the abuse. We believe the victim/survivor and we make this stance clear to the family.

• We do not encourage the abuser and survivor to be in a family session together until:

. the abuser is prepared to take full responsibility for the abuse, recognises the harm the abuse has caused the survivor, and is able to apologise to the survivor; and

. the survivor is ready for such a session and has a support person with her/him.

• We do not see the family with the 'hidden' agenda of them staying together or of the couple staying together. We are interested in helping family members to resolve relationship issues between each other, not to making 'happy families'. Nor are we interested in woman-blaming or victim-blaming.

- We believe prevention is very important. Abuser/victim roles can be repeated if the abuse cycle is not broken. If an abuser does not have to face responsibility for the abuse, he is likely to find another situation where he does the same again.

- All family members are affected by the abuse. The family experiences an emotional trauma. Only if the emotional issues are resolved in the family will there be some healing. When the abuser takes responsibility for the abuse, recognises the harm he has caused the victim/survivor and apologises, a great deal of healing can begin for the victim and for the other members of the family. We see individual work as being very important in this healing process. Individual work helps people work through their emotional pain and hurt and to think about family relationships. Work with different combinations of family members and family sessions is also very important in the healing process, and may help people work through the pain in those relationships. Group work is also useful, for example, in the healing process for the abuser, the confrontation and support from peers is a powerful way of offenders taking responsibility for their behaviour.

MAKING SENSE OF ABUSE:
A THEORY OF RESTRAINT

The cybernetic ideas of therapy have influenced our practice, particularly the notions of Bateson as applied by Michael White (1986).

By 'cybernetic' we mean that a negative explanation of events is preferred over a positive or 'dormative' description. This means that events take their course because they are restrained from alternative directions, as opposed to a belief that internal forces or compulsions drive events in a certain way. Negative explanation asks 'what stops an individual or the family from doing something differently'. It establishes a curiosity as to what has restrained family members from participation in alternative interactions and solutions.

According to Bateson, restraints act in relation to information about difference. They establish a threshold for the perception of news of difference. The therapist's task is to elicit information which gets over those thresholds and invites change.

Restraints of economies of alternatives - refer to the financial and social resources available which may restrain change from occurring. These are important considerations for women and children.

Restraints of redundancy - refer to the internal matrix of a person's world view - their values, beliefs and inner-programming. These restraints are not limited to individuals or families, but operate at a wider societal level.

For the victim, we may ask, 'what stops this person from surviving the trauma of violence or abuse?' Possible restraints may include:
- the violence or abuse is still occurring;
- the parent or family member remains in the family and is not accepting responsibility for the violence or abuse;
- trust has been shattered for the child or young person;
- the abused person may be invited to entertain ideas that they are to blame, that it was their fault, that they are now imperfect, unworthy and powerless and deserving of punishment.

For the abuser, we may ask, 'what stops this man taking responsibility for his actions?' Restraints may include:
- the patriarchial values of control, power and dominance;
- that fathers or adult men have rights over families; and
- that sexuality and male power are interlinked in today's society.

For the protecting parent (usually the mother), we may ask, 'what stops her from protecting her daughter?' Restraints may include:
- the power of the perpetrator to silence other members of the family;
- the woman's own history of being sexually or violently abused;
- the lack of emotional, financial and practical support;
- issues about how women survive alone in our society without the protection of men;
- fear of retribution, of violence and of being alone.

For society generally, we could ask the same question based on a negative explanation of events. 'What stops violence and abuse from being dealt with more effectively?' Restraints are numerous:
- lack of skill/knowledge about dealing with violence and abuse; the

justice system which acts as a deterrent against more reporting and prosecuting;

- the power of the family unit to close ranks to protect itself;
- social control (who deals and wields power in our society?);
- dismal alternatives - foster care, separation, removal of child which further victimises her/him;
- the loss of a breadwinner if the male is forced to leave;
- the struggle for women to survive without a partner and to bring up children single-handed.

PRINCIPLES OF THERAPY

- We believe it is important to make the therapeutic context a safe place for things to be said and to ensure people do not get hurt. For example, the question of the safety of women from pressure, threats or potential violence if they tell their partners (the abusers) they want to end the relationship. We try to make the therapy session a safe place for those things to be said and to ensure her safety in the future.

- Therapists may easily, but inadvertently, reflect the patterns of the family with whom they are working. In families where sexual abuse has occurred, power struggles are an issue. It is important for a therapy team to be conscious of these patterns so that they do not end up struggling over the same things, either between themselves or with the family.

- Gender appropriate therapy is important, especially for women who have been sexually abused. Healing through therapy is more likely to occur for someone who has been hurt and victimised if the therapist is not the same gender as the person who hurt them.

- Networking with families needs constant managing. There are difficulties in networking between agencies but the vision that all family members have the opportunity of participating in therapy to assist their healing process often means inter-agency networking.

- Each family is unique. We have similar goals for each family we see but the process is different.

- Sexual abuse is a compulsive behaviour that is gender related. Work with the abusers needs to focus on this in treatment.

CASE EXAMPLE (from Irene Esler)

Anne: A story of overcoming a victim lifestyle.

My colleague, Susan Bolt[1], had been seeing this woman for several months as part of an antenatal programme attached to an obstetric hospital. Anne was leaving the city and moving to the country. Susan asked me to join her in making a video tape to give Anne to mark her termination of therapy and to record her journey from victim to survivor.

In hindsight, what we were doing was recruiting an audience to her story. The ideas of Michael White and David Epston (1989) have been particularly helpful in understanding the importance of storying and re-authoring people's lives.

This young woman's story had been previously neglected. Her experience of her life had not been validated by her family or friends or the professionals she had encountered. Her story is one of protest and struggle to survive the overwhelming odds of continuing a victim lifestyle.

My purpose in seeing Anne was to help plot the course of her journey from a victim to a survivor - to allow her to tell her own story, discover her own journey and author her own life. On the way, I discovered that Anne was a remarkable young woman, resilient and strong, caring and gentle. This is her story of survival.

Anne's Story.

I am 28 years old. I am 7 months pregnant to John, my partner of one year. I have a daughter, Natasha, who is 7 years old. When I was 18, I got pregnant and gave the baby up for adoption at 3 months. I gave my first child up for adoption because I believed the woman would keep in touch. It was a private arrangement, I didn't go through the welfare, but the family went back on their word and took Becky away to another town. I know that one day Becky will want to find me and I'll be waiting for her when she does. I still have a lot of hurt about all that.

My parents split up when I was a baby. The family of 7 brothers and sisters were sent to different homes. The abuse started when I was 3 or 4, perhaps younger than 3. I was abused in most of the foster homes I lived in throughout my childhood. When the folk got sick of us, or if they wanted to go away somewhere for a holiday, you'd be palmed off on to someone else.

I was a chronic bedwetter. I got hidings every day for wetting my bed. I can remember in this particular Family Home, there'd be three of us lined up to get our hiding, then we'd have to wash our sheets before going to school. I was five at the time. This happened nearly every day.

The interference by males did me a lot of damage. It started very young. I remember the man next door taking me under his house and doing things to me. I told my foster mother at the time what had happened and she locked me in my bedroom for a week. She said I was making it up and she didn't believe me. I was abused off and on over my whole childhood. My mother married again and I went back home to live. My step-father never troubled me but two years ago I was feeling really sick with the flu and I couldn't cope with Natasha - so I went back home to Mum's. Mum wasn't there but my step-father was. He had never touched me before, the first male who hadn't, just about, and it was probably because I was sick that he took advantage of me. That really changed me. I just cried. You go home for security and you trust this guy. What's worse I was an adult, like I wasn't a child, yet I still let it happen to me. I didn't tell Mum. It's not worth it ...

Part of the session:

Anne: *It was after that incident that I thought 'hell, I'm not going to stay a victim all my life'.*

IE: *So how did you manage to turn the tide, how did you stop yourself from drowning in all this?*

Anne: *Because I wanted to. I have Natasha - she's important to me. I tell myself I'm important and sometimes this works.*

IE: *Do you think in some way, that it is your fault?*

Anne: *It has always been my fault. That's what I've been told.*

IE: *Do you believe that?*

Anne: *I know it's not, but it's what other people think of you.*

IE: *And what do you think of yourself? Does that count too?*

Anne: *Yes, I know that inside I'm a good person, a gentle person. I don't like hurting people. This is my downfall. I let people walk all over me. I don't care how much I get hurt as long as other people don't.*

IE: *What happens when you taken on other people's hurt? Has it sapped your strength for yourself?*

Anne: *Oh yes, definitely. I don't understand why I am a strong person. I know I am to have survived all that hurt from the past. But I don't really know where that strength comes from. Deep down I know what sort of person I am, but I'm not letting that person come out.*

IE: *What would help to let that person out?*

Anne: *I don't know.*

IE: *It seems to me that you're starting to see yourself in a different way.*

Anne: *Yes, I am.*

IE: *What other signs have there been for you that tell you you are seeing yourself in a different way?*

Anne: *There was an incident at the Post Office when I went to get my benefit money. I asked for an update. The lady behind the counter said 'You're lucky you're getting this money at all'. It was as if she was saying - 'you're nothing, you don't deserve to get money'. Well, I spoke up for myself and told her what I thought of her. I walked out of there with my head high.*

IE: *It's easy to feel unworthy when you've been treated so badly as a child. That's amazing that you didn't just take it that time.*

Anne: *I've done a lot of re-thinking about those thoughts. How I see myself. I never thought I'd be able to change. I kept trusting people and they'd hurt me. But I made a decision not to continue to do that.*

IE: *How did you do that?*

Anne: *I know now that I can decide not to like people who have hurt me. I've cut off contact with those people. I've stopped being nice to them.*

IE: *Is that another marker on the way to becoming your own person?*

Anne: *Yes, I suppose it is.*

IE: *What other signs of strength do you notice?*

Anne: *Well, I tell my daughter to be strong. I wasn't believed as a child and I've told her that I will always believe her. I've told John, 'you'll only get the one chance. Touch her and that's it.'*

IE: *When did you start thinking of yourself as a survivor?*

Anne: *There have been dramatic changes when I think about it. But it's also a slow process.*

IE: *How did you encourage that strong part of you?*

Anne: *Other people let you down, you have to have a belief in yourself. I*

stand in front of the mirror and say: 'Come on Anne, get your bloody shit together.'
IE: *It seems to be a good formula!*
Anne: *I've accepted that there's nothing wrong with me. There was a different person there in the mirror.*
IE: *How are you facing the future and what do you think lies ahead?*
Anne: *There will be negative days as well as positive ones, I know that. But there has definitely been a turn-around.*
IE: *As you are moving into a survivor's lifestyle, do you experience more control in your life?*
Anne: *I tell myself those thoughts belong in the past, the future belongs to me. I still feel a lot of hurt towards my mother and brothers and sisters. My hurt is very deep.*
IE: *How does that hurt show?*
Anne: *Well, I found it really hard to put my arms around my daughter. I'd make excuses not to cuddle her. Just lately, I have been able to go up to her, not all the time, just sometimes, and I can give her a cuddle, or I can say to her 'give me a cuddle'. I've always been a good mother to Natasha, never hurt her or pushed her away, or anything like that. But now, things are changing, starting to improve.*
IE: *Sounds like there's a new dimension in your relationship with Natasha that wasn't there before?*
Anne: *Yes, there is and it's exciting ...*

Conclusion:

Anne's last words as we said goodbye:
'I feel a strong sense from you that you were really interested in me. Sometimes people don't really want to know your story. But I sensed that Susan, over these last few months, was always genuinely interested, and today both of you have listened and cared about my story. I feel I can put it behind me now.'

CASE EXAMPLE (from Jane Waldegrave)

Major influences behind my work are the Milan Group; the work of Peggy Papp and Olga Silverstein; Michael White's and David Epston's ideas; the Rochdale Team's[2] work on networking; more recently, Amanda Kamsler's work; and my experience of working with referrals from the state welfare department, where a larger system has a huge influence on a family.

In therapy, I am particularly interested in relationship patterns in the family, the effects of the past on relationships in the family and the effects of family beliefs on relationships. I'm interested in the family finding their own strengths by understanding what's been happening and what that means for them, and doing so from a position of survival. This will contribute to their healing and help them discover resources they have for the future.

The Rochdale Team's ideas on networking show the importance of getting all those who are involved in the problem (workers and family) together to talk to each other in a way that is empowering and contributes to resolving the problem. I've used these ideas to fit the New Zealand Department of Social Welfare scene. Often families have the types of problems that involve many and various issues, and these complexities require the appropriate people to talk together. Often this involves meeting with different groups of professionals. It can seem like slowly walking through a swamp and getting to the other side, rather than sinking into it and drowning.

How one implements each stage in therapy influences, and is a model for relationship patterns within the family's system and within the family and therapist system. If this first part is not done effectively, it makes the following parts more difficult. Acknowledging the abuse and changing relationship patterns go together.

The therapy team has to be careful that it does not inadvertently mirror the family patterns of relating. The power struggles that are inevitable in families where there is sexual abuse are strongly ingrained in their relationship patterns. Working with these families exposes the therapists to these patterns in a very real way, for example, patterns of gender imbalance and power differences.

The Wilson Family: A healing process through therapy.

A colleague and I were seeing families of some of the men in an Adult Sexual Offenders Group, run by Stephen Jacobs (my colleague) and

Dr Fred Seymour. The agency is the Specialist Services Unit, Department of Social Welfare (DSW). This means that a DSW social worker also has to be involved with the family for us to see them. In this case, the mother of the abused young woman had reported the abuse to a DSW social worker.

We have two major goals in our work with such a family. One is that we aim to assist the abuser to a point where he will take responsibility for what he has done, be able to acknowledge the harm he has caused, and to apologise. For the abuser to be able to attend the Adult Sexual Offenders Group, he has to have admitted he is a sexual abuser. Although a start, this does not necessarily mean that he is taking responsibility for the harm he has done.

The second aim is to involve the rest of the family and provide an opportunity to go through a healing process by attending therapy. We put considerable effort into helping them claim their own power and deal with their pain. It is clear that, from the victim's/survivor's point of view, if the abuser wants to build up a relationship with her/him, nothing can happen until he takes that step of taking responsibility for the abuse, acknowledging the harm he has caused and apologising.

The following case study is a long story of how a family worked through the trauma of sexual abuse. The offender (husband, stepfather, and father) is not fully part of this process because, once he'd completed the Adult Sexual Offenders Group sessions which he agreed to attend, he did not want to be involved further in therapy. He has not been part of the original household since the beginning of therapy. When 'family' is mentioned, it is mostly referring to the new family of mother and children.

The Wilson Family.

Brian (husband/father/stepfather) had sexually abused Prue (15) over a period of several years, and Rosemary (10) once, about four years ago. Prue told her mother, Louise, who had acted immediately. She took Prue to the police station that same night. Rosemary also disclosed abuse. Brian was approached by the police and admitted to sexually abusing Prue but said he 'could not remember' abusing Rosemary. Brian left the home and agreed to attend an Adult Sexual Abusers Group for thirteen weeks, one evening per week.

There are two other children in the family, Sarah (6) and Thomas (4), who are Louise and Brian's children. Prue and Rosemary are children from Louise's first marriage. Louise and Brian have been together for seven years.

The first contact with the family was a 'contract meeting' held as a pre-entry requirement to the Sexual Abuser Group. Part of the contract included that the family have sessions according to their needs. There was no compulsion for Louise or the young women to meet with Brian. Brian had to attend sessions if Louise asked him to do so.

Louise would not attend this contract meeting because she thought therapy was a 'soft option to get Brian off the charges'. I visited Louise a week later with the contract, to explain it to her and to work out a way for her and the children to begin a healing process by attending therapy for themselves.

The family holds strong religious beliefs. Their church was supporting Brian and was pressuring Louise to forgive him. Louise thought it would be good to have a religious counsellor for herself because she and her daughters were grappling with issues around their faith, and a Christian counsellor agreed to see Louise, Prue and Rosemary individually for sexual abuse counselling. It was arranged that I would be the case manager and work with the family along with another colleague.

I arranged a family meeting with Louise and her four children two weeks later. The Christian counsellor was present and was introduced to the family at this session. The other purpose of this meeting was to help them to adjust to being a 'new' family, and to help them deal with coming to terms with the trauma of sexual abuse.

What happened in the session and issues that arose.

The main focus of the session was their worries at home and their opinions about why their step-father/father/husband wasn't living in the house. We talked about ways the family discuss what Brian had done to Prue and Rosemary.

Some new connections were made for the children about what had happened. The youngest child had no idea why his father wasn't there and the family group had no language to describe what had happened, even though the three older children had a clear understanding of why Brian was absent. By talking about it more openly, they came to an agreement that they could refer to it as 'Brian had been doing very frightening things to Prue and Rosemary in their beds'. We referred to the sexual abuse in this language from then on. The older girls wanted to have a phrase they could use to explain Brian's absence to their friends.

As regards their worries, Louise was worried about Sarah having nightmares and being hyperactive; she was concerned that Sarah may have been sexually abused as well. She was also worried about Thomas being 'angry' and having terrible tantrums. She wanted information and methods to deal with this. The older girls also had these worries, and were especially concerned about the possibility that Sarah had been sexually abused.

Louise talked about her own abuse by a non-family member when she was 5 years old. She and Prue and Rosemary had talked about this recently.

Louise had a very clear stance that Brian was responsible for the abuse and that it was 'totally inexcusable' - she didn't think he was remorseful and she wanted to end the relationship for good. She spoke about this with the children and the two older girls were very relieved.

What seemed clear from this session was that Brian was not taking responsibility for his behaviour, acknowledging the harm he had caused, or apologising. In the contract session and in the Adult Group he was saying the 'right' things. However, Louise was clear that in her dealings with him he was still justifying himself and had not accepted responsibility for the abuse to herself or to the girls.

Our goals at this stage were:
- to deal with the issue of Brian taking responsibility for the abuse;
- to set up appropriate therapy sessions for Louise and the children;
- to help Louise resolve her relationship with Brian.

What happened next.

An evidential interview was set up for Sarah, and individual counselling was underway with Louise, Prue and Rosemary.

Brian had pleaded 'guilty' in court and was given two years probation rather than a prison sentence. The church pastor had put forward a convincing argument to the court. Brian was now attending the Adult Sexual Abusers Group.

Three weeks after the court's decision, a meeting was set up between Brian and Louise to discuss their future as a couple. Louise wanted to be clear with Brian that she wished to end the relationship. She also wanted to address with Brian the issue of the church pressuring her to forgive him. Brian wanted to talk about their relationship and his relationship to the children, and access issues. Each of them was invited to bring a support person/s to this session and each did so - Brian was accompanied by his lawyer, and Louise brought an old friend.

By the time Louise arrived at the session, she was clear where she stood and what she wanted. Her support person was to help her articulate this.

When a woman wants to tell her partner (who is an abuser) that she wants to end the relationship, the therapist faces a number of important questions. How safe is the woman from pressure, threats, or potential violence if she says this to her partner? It is important to make the therapeutic context a safe place for these things to be said and to ensure her safety in the future. However, it is an issue because it's not always possible to ensure her safety. And yet, with the relationship unresolved, he is hassling her and she is frightened. Our aim is to support them in resolving their relationship, for fear of violence if the situation remains the same. Otherwise we are condoning the abuser to continue having 'power over' his wife and the children.

What happened in this session and issues that arose.

At the beginning of this session, we made a statement about Louise and Brian being unclear about what was happening between them in their relationship. There were also some misunderstandings about Brian's relationship with Prue and Rosemary and with the two younger children.

We asked Louise to talk from her point of view. (She knew this was going to happen and had agreed to this procedure.)

Louise spoke about the trust being broken and was very clear that she was no longer wanting a relationship with him. Brian found this hard to hear and accept. He said he hoped she would change her mind and that what she was saying now was only temporary. She was clear with him that she did not want him to have this hope, that she was sure about not wanting a relationship with him. He talked about miracles happening.

When we asked him about that, it led into a discussion on the issue of the church pressuring her to forgive him because the church believed he had the right to go back into the home since he had repented. In this way she became the sinner in the church's eyes. We asked her where she stood with this view and she was able to say that, in her view, he was not remorseful, he had not accepted responsibility for the abuse, had not acknowledged the harm he had caused the two girls, and the rest of the family, had not apologised to the girls and that she had the right to say she wanted to end the relationship. Stephen used this material with Brian in the session to encourage him and his lawyer (also a church member) to understand that repentance was not enough and that Louise and the young women were being further victimised by the church's attitude. Stephen confronted them in a respectful way and acted as a bridge between the two attitudes. The lawyer was more convinced than Brian and was useful in helping to persuade Brian. Finally, Brian accepted the situation and agreed to write a letter of apology to Prue and Rosemary. (By this time he had 'remembered' that he had abused Rosemary as well.) He also agreed to make a statement to the congregation about what he had done and that he wanted to take the blame for his marriage breaking up. He was also saying he accepted that Louise wanted to end the relationship.

It is important that the therapists have an agreement that it is the abuser who should change his stance, rather than the victims/survivors. Often it is the abuser who has traditionally stood his ground in the household and family, while his wife and children manoeuvered around him. To try to get him to do the manoeuvering is politically sound and therapeutic for the family. He is responsible for the damage in the family so he must do the 'moving' in terms of his beliefs: practical details like moving out of the house rather than the survivor, and working out what he can do to show he has taken responsibility for the abuse.

This led to the issue of Brian's relationship with the older girls and access with his two children. Louise stated that Prue and Rosemary did not ever want to see him again. The court had ruled that he have no access with them. She would only agree to supervised access to Sarah and Thomas. Brian was shocked and went through a similar process of pressuring Louise by making out she was victimising him and complaining that he didn't deserve this sort of treatment. She spoke about trust issues and the closeness between all four children. Again Stephen worked with

Brian with this material. (Often the mother/partner is not as clear as Louise was able to be, and we have to present the issues to the abuser.) He finally agreed and we worked out who would supervise his access visits and how often and how they could be organized.

This was one of the first times Louise had been assertive and able to claim her own power. This was a change from the old pattern of Brian withdrawing and Louise being loud, to a new pattern of Brian listening and Louise being clear.

What happened next.

Sarah's evidential interview revealed that Brian had not abused her but that another family friend had several years before. Procedures against the abuser were started and therapy for Sarah began.

Brian had finished the 13 week programme with the Adult Sexual Abuse Group. The contract stipulates we have a Review Meeting once the 13 weeks are through. A meeting was set up for this.

The individual counselling for Louise and the two older girls broke down. The girls only attended one session and Louise only two. Our expectations had been that all three would have the opportunity to work through the pain of the abuse. I thought this had been carefully negotiated with their counsellor, but obviously there were some misunderstandings.

Louise had a session with me to clarify what she wanted to say at the Review Meeting as to whether Brian had made 'real' changes. That session helped her be clear about what she thought and also prepared her for what could be a difficult session. She only attends sessions if she wants to and is ready to confront him. This is a useful strategy to help him towards being responsible for his behaviour.

We were wanting to use this Review Meeting to further achieve these goals.

The Review Meeting.
What happened in the session and issues that arose.

Louise and two support people (the same friend who attended the previous session, and her sister-in-law - Brian's brother's wife), Brian and his support person (not his lawyer, instead the man with whom he was boarding who also belonged to the church), and Brian's Probation Officer, attended the session.

Each person was asked about changes they had noticed since the contract meeting with regard to Brian and how he sees things now with the abuse, his behaviour, and his relationships with family members. Is Brian safe to be around others? Has he really changed? For an abuser to become aware of his sexist and patriarchal beliefs and practices in therapy is no easy task. As part of this, he must get to a point where he accepts responsibility for the abuse, acknowledges the damage he has done to the survivor and the rest of the family, and apologises to the survivor. For this to happen requires change at a deep level. How can this be judged? Who can tell? This problem is one of secrecy and trickery. To be clear it has changed is difficult to prove.

In our experience, the abuser's partners and the survivors know whether he has really changed. They can tell by a look or a comment. Prue knew with her letter that Brian had not changed a bit. Louise knew the games he played and could spot them very easily. These women are experts because they have lived in the confusion of 'he's a nice guy/he's treacherous' for years. When they have unravelled things for themselves they have learnt to trust their own intuitions. They are the most likely to know when he's playing tricks.

In the session, Brian said he had accepted that his couple relationship with Louise was over. He had kept to his agreements regarding access to the children, and these visits were going well.

Although Brian was saying he was admitting openly now that what he had done was 'totally wrong', Louise said he hadn't really changed because she thought he was still blaming his behaviour on herself and the girls by justifying what he did. Brian had not written a letter to each of the girls apologising for the abuse as he had promised to do. Brian's support person did not agree with Louise about him justifying his behaviour. Louise's support people had not had much to do with Brian over the last 3 months so it was difficult for them to notice changes. Louise hadn't seen much of him either. She had heard the justifications through friends and, because the promised letters hadn't arrived, she thought he wasn't taking responsibility for what he'd done. By not sending the letters, Louise explained, he had further hurt the girls because they had been waiting for them.

Also, Brian had not made a statement to the congregation about it being his behaviour that had caused their marriage to break up. This was another reason for Louise to believe he had not taken responsibility for the abuse. Discussing the different opinions about Brian justifying his behaviour revealed that he had 'forgotten' to write but was very willing to write this week. He said he had approached the pastor who had not agreed to Brian making a statement to the congregation. Brian and his support person reiterated again that Brian wanted to be responsible for what he had done. Louise said she was suspicious but would wait for the letters to arrive.

The issue of the church's attitude was further discussed. Brian's support person was a respected church member. Stephen challenged him about whether the church recognised Brian's problem and was able to prevent him from re-abusing or did the church dismiss the abuse and cocoon Brian? I challenged him on how the church had not backed Louise but the law had: Brian and his support person accepted the importance of what was being said as did the Probabtion Officer. It was decided between us that a meeting be set up with the pastor of the church to discuss these issues. The meeting would be about the influence of the church's attitudes on Brian.

We saw that it was imperative that this be addressed next because the church's influence had the greatest influence on Brian. Louise's reality was being believed for the first time about this issue. It is important for her that she was being heard and believed.

What happened next.

Brian sent a letter to each of the girls. He had agreed to read them to the Abusers Group before he sent them. He did and the group told him that one letter was good, the other one wasn't, and that he should re-write the 'not-so-good' one. He sent them without changes. Rosemary's response to her letter was positive and Louise thought it had had a healing effect on her. Prue's response to her letter was, 'it doesn't mean a thing to me', and she became really upset.

A date was set for a meeting with the pastor. Louise decided to attend a group for mothers of children who have been sexually abused. Louise was concerned about Prue's introvertedness and requested a session with herself and Prue to help Prue be more outgoing. A time was made for that.

Rosemary asked to attend therapy with the Art Therapist that Sarah was seeing.

The session with Louise, Prue, and Rosemary, three weeks after the Review Meeting: what happened in the session and issues that arose.

I worked on my own in this session. The family agreed that I video it. I decided to suggest that Rosemary attend the session with Louise and Prue. The focus of the session was to be on Louise and Prue's relationship, and the effect Brian's abusive behaviour had had on that relationship. Prue's relationship with her mother was different from Rosemary's relationship with Louise. How was this so when Brian has abused both the girls? It made sense to have both girls at the session to see how the effect of the abuse was different for each young woman and how it had differently affected their relationships with their mother. These new understandings would also go some way to improving the sisters' relationship.[3]

I planned to talk about the history of closeness in their mother/daughter relationships before the abuse, during the abusive period and since, and the silencing effect that the abuse has had on their relationships. I wanted to ask questions like: 'How did his intimidating you affect your relationship with your mother/sister? How has his trickery with you affected your relationship with each other?' I also wanted to underline the love between mother and daughter.

Some excerpts from the session, showing the effect Brian's abusive behaviour had on the mother/daughter relationships.

Therapist: *Can you remember a time before Brian joined the family when you felt close? I'm asking you this so that I can understand what your experience was as young women before Brian was part of the household.*
Prue: *We were always close.*
Therapist: *How were you close?*
Prue: *I could talk to mum about everything.*
Therapist: *Has it gone back to that closeness since Brian has been out of the household?*
Prue: *Not really.*
Therapist: (to Louise) *Can you remember the closeness you had with each*

other before you got together with Brian?

Louise: *We were close.*

We established that Brian's abusive behaviour stopped them talking much to each other. I talked about this as Brian's behaviour having the effect of silencing them and thus putting a gap between them. The following excerpt addresses the effect of that gap in relation to their not telling Louise about the abuse.

Therapist: (to Rosemary) *How do you think Brian silencing you affected your relationship with your mother? What stopped you from telling her?*

Rosemary: *I was scared she wouldn't believe me. I thought Brian would coach her into not believing me and then I'd get punished for not telling the truth. That might break my relationship with my mother because she'd think badly of me. She'd think I'm a liar.*

Therapist: *It was important to you not to break your relationship with your mother. You didn't want to put anything in the way of that relationship with her. Him silencing you was one way Brian's behaviour has put a wedge between you and your mother.*

Rosemary: *I know that will never happen now because she did believe me.*

Therapist: *That was wonderful that Louise believed you. It's what Brian did that caused the wedge.*

Therapist: *Prue, how has Brian's abusing you affected your relationship with your mother? What stopped you from telling?*

Prue: *I thought I'd break up her marriage. I didn't talk to her much. Everything I told mum she told him so I didn't tell her anything. I kept all those things and feelings to myself. I thought it might destroy Mum's life if I told. I thought she might not manage.*

Further questions and discussion of this showed the extent to which the young women thought Brian had influenced their mother not believing them and caused a wedge in their relationships that had lasted for six or so years. His trickery had led them to believe this. It had also led Louise to worry and watch Prue grow up and grow away from her.

It was clear how important and precious their mother/daughter relationships were to each of them. Also, I was impressed with how strong the young women had been to have survived this time of abuse and silence, and how strong Louise was to have survived the guilt and shame of her husband abusing her daughters, her marriage break-up, being able to cope on her own with four children, and the loss of her church affiliations.

The last part of the session looked at their relationships now. Prue said she still couldn't talk to her mother about everything. We talked about the wedge having gone but a gap having been left. Prue had developed a way of coping over the years by being quiet. Prue's quietness was put in the context of needing time to recover from the years of intrusion and fear from the abuse. She was establishing her own sense of safety and it would take time. Trust was a big issue. Louise understood and agreed.

I sent a letter after this session to the three of them, reiterating the things we'd talked about in the session, and underlining how Brian's abusive behaviour had had an enormous affect on the closeness of their relationships.

I believe the session and the letter brought some understanding about the pain and hurt they have suffered and still are suffering, and also some understanding that would free them from guilt and shame.

What happened next.

A week later a meeting was held with Brian, the pastor, the church person with whom Brian was boarding, and with Stephen Jacobs as the therapist/facilitator. Stephen reported later that the pastor continued to support Brian, and condone his abusive behaviour. It would take more than a meeting to change that.

Rosemary and Sarah both attended separate art therapy sessions - Sarah for ten sessions, and Rosemary for seven. As a finishing ritual for the girls, the art therapist, Carol Sedgewick, and myself ran a Family Art Therapy session that Louise and her four children attended. We sent them a letter following the session about the issues that arose. This session was held two months after the Review Session, and five months since the beginning of therapy.

Louise had six individual sessions with me for ongoing support to look at her own issues. These lasted a further four months. Prue didn't want to attend any more sessions and only reluctantly attended the Family Art Therapy session.

A meeting was held, two months after the Family Art Therapy session, with a Police Indecency Squad Sergeant regarding the man who sexually abused Sarah. (This had been delayed because the police had lost the file.) Louise and Brian attended and so did Sarah's Art Therapist. Plans were made regarding his arrest. Prue and Rosemary had witnessed the abuse on one occasion and were subsequently interviewed. Brian was angry at the session that Sarah had been abused. Sarah is his natural daughter. We made some links with him about Louise's anger at him having abused her other two daughters.

Louise requested a meeting with the caregivers. The caregivers are the three families who have agreed to make their homes and their supervision available for Brian to visit with Sarah and Thomas. There had been some problems with one of the caregivers (a fourth family that no longer participates as a caregiver family), and Louise wanted to be clear about ground rules with the existing caregivers. These were made and some misunderstandings cleared up.

Brian had been suspected of doing some 'peeping' but had not been caught. He is currently living in a caravan in the church grounds.

At follow up: a year since the first contact with the family.

Louise says the family are fine. Sarah and Thomas are doing well - they are settled and happy. They are much easier to handle.

Prue and Louise's mother/daughter relationship is going much more smoothly. Prue is sharing more of her worries with her mother. She has stopped hiding things from Louise and talks about what she is doing. She is going out socializing and coping well with that. Louise says that Prue still has a 'negative self image' and Louise sometimes worries about that, but she is not 'living her life for her any more'. Louise is very happy to have a closer relationship with Prue now.

Rosemary is growing taller and having 'crushes on boys'.

Louise has a special friend who is a male and she talks about looking after herself in the relationship. Trusting a friendship is something she didn't think she'd ever do again. She is taking things slowly and carefully. She is happy about how things are going.

Louise says that it's so important for her that she and her daughters can talk to each other about almost anything. It's what she'd hoped for and what she had missed out on with her own mother. That's been an important outcome of the therapy for her.

NOTES

1. Social Worker in Melbourne - previously in Auckland, New Zealand.

2. The Rochdale Team's ideas on networking are referred to in Morrison (1987). See also Dale et al (1986) in References.

3. I want to acknowledge Amanda Kamsler's very helpful ideas in this area of work (1989/90). I also want to acknowledge Kate Kowalski's excellent article (Kowalski 1987/88). She talks about the therapist having an assumption that the '... mother/daughter relationship is a meaningful one to both, therefore treatment should work to enhance their participation in a positive direction.' Kowalski's article provides a very good therapeutic foundation for working with mothers and daughters.

REFERENCES

Dale, P., Davies, M., Morrison, T. & Waters, J. 1986:
Dangerous Families. Tavistock.
Dimmock, B. & Dungworth, D. 1985:
'Beyond the family: using network meetings with statutory child care cases."
Australian Journal of Family Therapy, 7:45-68.
Kamsler, A. 1989/90:
Training workshops for therapists working with women who were sexually a-bused in childhood, and with mothers and children where sexual abuse has been disclosed. Christchurch & Auckland, New Zealand.
Kamsler, A. 1990:
'The story of Alice: an illustration of the therapy process, in Her-story in the making.'
Ideas for Therapy with Sexual Abuse. Adelaide, Dulwich Centre Publications.
Kowalski, K. 1987/88:
'The importance of mothers in the treatment of sexually abused adolescent girls.'
Dulwich Centre Newsletter, Summer.
Morrison, T. 1987:
'Professional dangerousness and networking". Seminar.
Palazzoli, M.S., Boscolo, L., Cecchin, G. & Prata, G. 1980:
'Hypothesising - circularity - neutrality: three guidelines for the conductor of the session.' **Family Process**, 19(1):3-12.
Palazzoli, M.S., Boscolo, L., Cecchin, G. & Prata, G. 1981:
Paradox and Counter-paradox. New York, Aronson.
Papp, P. 1983:
The Process of Change. New York, Guildford.
Walters, M., Carter, B., Papp, P. & Silverstein, O. 1988:
The Invisible Webb: Gender patterns in family relationships. New York, Guildford.

White, M. 1986:
    'Negative explanation, restraint & double description: a template for family thera-
    py.'**Family Process**, 25:2.
White, M. 1988:
    'The process of questioning: a therapy of literary merit?'**Dulwich Centre News-
    letter**, Winter.
White, M. 1988/89:
    'The externalizing of the problem.'**Dulwich Centre Newsletter**, Summer.
White, M. & Epston, D. 1989:
    Literate Means to Therapeutic Ends. Adelaide, Dulwich Centre Publications.

CHAPTER VI

PUTTING AN END

to

SECRECY

Therapy with mothers and children
following disclosure
of
child sexual assault

by

Lesley Laing
&
Amanda Kamsler

This chapter discusses an approach to therapy with mothers and children, following the disclosure of intrafamilial child sexual assault. While specifically addressing the situation where the offender is in a parental role, either biological or social, with respect to the victim/s, many of the ideas are applicable to situations where the offender is not a father figure, but was able to assault a child by virtue of his position of trust in the child's family. The focus of the chapter is on ongoing therapy, rather than crisis intervention at the time of disclosure.

The therapeutic approach described here derives from the work of Michael White (1988, 1988/89, 1989), and from feminist writers (Rush 1980; Herman 1981; Ward 1984). While some clinicians are using similar ideas in work with men who are violent and with perpetrators of sexual assault, this chapter considers therapy with mothers and children in situations where the parents have separated as a result of the sexual assault.

Until quite recently, incest was regarded as an extremely rare problem, which occurred in only few grossly deviant families. Only in the last ten or so years has the true extent of the problem begun to be revealed (Waldby 1985; Russell 1986; Goldman & Goldman 1988).

Lifting the veil of secrecy which has kept the problem of incest hidden can be largely attributed to the feminist movement. Feminist analyses (Rush 1980; Herman 1981; Ward 1984) have located the existence of incest in the way in which gender relationships are structured in society, and argue that the problem cannot be understood outside this societal context. Alan Jenkins (1988) describes the societal context in which incest occurs as one in which there is a 'gendered imbalance of power and responsibility', which creates a 'blueprint for the oppression of women and children'.

THE LITERATURE: THE INVISIBLE OFFENDER

While some of the clinical literature reflects awareness of the wider social context within which incest occurs (e.g Herman 1981), this is the exception rather than the rule.

More pervasive is an approach which regards the family in which incest has occurred as 'dysfunctional' without analysis of the societal context in which notions about the family and the roles of its members   are constructed. This way of thinking is highly influential in informing the practice of treatment programmes which have served as models for intervention with families in which incest has occurred, such as the programme developed by the Giarettos in Santa Clara County, California. *Incest can be regarded as a symptom of a dysfunctional family: a family headed by parents who are unable to develop a satisfying marital relationship and who cannot co-operate effectively as parents. (Giaretto 1982, p.4)*

The typical scenario presented is one in which the marital relationship is poor, the mother copes by withdrawing either physically or emotionally, the daughter is propelled by the mother's withdrawal into a 'parental' role and responsibilities, and the father turns to his daughter sexually because of his wife's failure to meet his needs. For example:

Refusal to have intercourse with one's husband, setting up one's daughter's bedroom next to the husband's, requiring the daughter to take over household duties, being absent from the house, are all covert but unambiguous messages both to the husband and the daughter that the daughter is to assume some of the functions normally exercised by the wife. (Machotka et al 1967, p.110)

Typically, this scenario is uncritically accepted as describing the breakdown of the 'normal' family, without analysis of the underlying sexist assumptions about 'normal' sex roles. (For example, the male's right to have his sexual needs fulfilled, and if not by his wife then by his daughter as most available female; household tasks as the domain of women and girls; etc.)

Most of the literature which takes a 'family dysfunction' approach is either overtly or covertly mother blaming. For example, in analysis of a number of families in which incest had occurred, Lustig et al conclude:

Despite the overt culpability of the fathers, we were impressed with their psychological passivity in the transactions leading to incest. The mother appeared the cornerstone in the pathological family system. (1966, p.39)

This is echoed more recently by Sgroi:

For their part, the women often tended to be 'psychologically absent' in their relationships with both their husbands and their children. They seemed to exhibit a lack of psychological investment in the interpersonal aspect of their marriage and family lives. (1982, p.193)

The mother's role as emotional caretaker and protector of children is assumed to be the norm, and is unquestioned.

Of course, the father has an important role to play in the rearing of well-

balanced children, but the mother remains the essential and primary parent.
(Giaretto 1982, p.35)

Thus, when incest occurs, the mother assumes responsibility by virtue of her perceived abrogation of her maternal and wifely roles:

The mother may not always be aware of the sources of her guilt, but in time she usually will admit to strong wrenches of guilt for not fulfilling her role as mother and wife. If she had ministered to the needs of her family instead of her own selfish wants, the incestuous events would not have occurred, had she met her husband's emotional and sexual needs, he would not have turned to her daughter for satisfying them, had she kept her eyes and ears open, she would have caught the situation and been able to protect her daughter. (Giaretto 1982, p.37) - (emphasis added)

While some writers have exposed the many flaws in examining the mother's role through the lens of the 'dysfunctional family' (McIntyre 1981; Wattenburg 1985), there is evidence that ideas about the 'dysfunctional family' remain highly influential in informing practice with families (Dietz & Craft 1980; MacFarlane & Waterman 1986).

A consequence of the family dysfunction approach is that the offender's role is rendered invisible: fathers who commit the crime of sexual assault become just one of the members of the dysfunctional 'incestuous family'. Mothers become responsible for being ill, pregnant, depressed and for failing to protect their children by not containing their partner's sexual drive. Never is it assumed that the male, as an adult, should be expected to take responsibility for ensuring that his behaviour towards children is appropriate and not exploitative or abusive. The spotlight is turned onto the mother in the search for an explanation of the incest:

For whatever combination of reasons, one of the characteristics of the 'psychologically absent' mothers of incest victims is to fail to protect by failing to limit inappropriate behaviour between their husbands and children. (Sgroi 1982, p.193)

In the search for the characteristics of the 'psychologically absent' mother, the role of the offender easily fades into the shadows.

Of note is the fact that uncles, brothers and other abusers of children who are trusted family members are even more invisible in this literature, despite evidence that they commit many acts of sexual assault on children (Russell 1986).

The implications of this approach for clinicians are confusing and contradictory. One area of contradiction is the question of responsibility for the sexual assault. On the one hand, the therapist is urged to work with the father towards his unconditional acceptance of responsibility for the sexual assault. However, the mother is also urged to assume responsibility, and **both** parents apologise to the child and explain:

... that the parents, and not the child, are responsible for the incest situation. (Horowitz 1983, p.521) - (emphasis added)

Therapeutic approaches which fail to take account of the wider social context in which incest occurs and which do not contain an analysis of power and responsibility are incomplete, and risk perpetuating problems of guilt, blame, secrecy and division in the relationships of mothers and children following the disclosure of incest. Secrecy is central to the existence of incest. By abusing his power behind a shield of secrecy, the offender is able to escape taking responsibility for his behaviour. We wish to propose an alternative approach which seeks to intervene in ways which are empowering to women and children.

THE OFFENDER'S SHIELD OF 'INVISIBILITY' AND THE CONSEQUENCES FOR THE MOTHER AND CHILD

Our approach to therapy with mothers and children is grounded in an appreciation of the offender's central role in shaping the beliefs and perceptions of the mother and victim/s about themselves, each other, and the issue of responsibility. The offender's role in this is obscured as a result of the kinds of beliefs current in society about why sexual assault happens and about who is responsible. (For example, the widely held view that children can be 'seductive' towards adults; and the idea that it is the responsibility of women to contain the sexual urges of men.) The offender's opportunity to shape the beliefs of the victim, in particular, lies in his role and power to enforce secrecy, which perpetuates a closed, unchallenged system until disclosure. We argue that secrecy is a central factor in making it possible for sexual assault to continue within the family.

The continued enforcement of secrecy is possible because of the offender's position as a parent and a male. It is also essential to enable the offender to continue to have access to his victim/s, and to enable him to avoid taking responsibility for his behaviour. Secrecy is enforced by the offender in a variety of ways, usually cleverly matched to 'fit' with the developmental age and emotional vulnerability of the child. With a very young child, the sexual contact may be presented as a special 'secret' game, while an adolescent may be threatened with loss of social freedoms if she tells. Violence towards the victim or other family members, family disruption, maternal breakdown and many other threats are commonly invoked to ensure the victim's compliance with the rule of secrecy.

Consequences for the Child

Secrecy enables the offender to avoid taking responsibility for the sexual assault. Typically, he denies responsibility for the assault, for its impact, and for the consequences to the rest of the family. A major ploy he uses to shift responsibility away from himself is to give the victim the message, either covertly or overtly, that the sexual contact is the child's fault. In our experience, children have reported being told things such as: 'I can't help myself when I see you.' 'You've let me do it for so long, who's going to believe you didn't want it?' 'You're a slut.' His efforts reflect and amplify the beliefs about responsibility for sexual assault of which the child may become aware in the wider society. (For example, rape victims must have led the man on.)

Interactions such as these with the offender will have far reaching consequences for the child. This shifting of responsibility from the offender to the child creates a context in which the child will experience feelings of guilt and shame about the sexual assault, and these feelings will create a further barrier to her ability to overcome secrecy. Additionally, as a result of the offender's encouragement to see herself as bad or as deserving this sort of treatment, the child may actually become convinced that she is an unlovable person. Self-hate is a likely effect of this. In our experience, many women presenting for therapy with symptoms such as self mutilation will frequently disclose a history of sexual assault.

Since the child's actual experience may be at variance with the offender's account of events (e.g. he may be saying 'You really like this' when she is experiencing pain and fear), she may be overwhelmed by an array of confusing feelings. She may become unsure of what she feels and this may result in her becoming right out of touch with herself. One of the strongest emotions which the child may experience is fear which originated

in the frightening secret interactions with the offender. For example:
Don't you say anything to your mother ever. If you do you'll be sorrier than you've ever been in your life. (Bass & Thornton 1983, p.77)
Fear may continue to dominate her life, for example, in nightmares.

By using the child for his own needs, the offender will have given the child a strong message to put his needs before her own. For example: 'You're the only one who really understands me'. This may have become a habit to the point where she may regularly put other people ahead of herself in a way which makes it hard for others to help and care for her. This can lay the foundation for a 'being for others' lifestyle.

All these feelings and habits of thought will affect the child's behaviour and contribute to the development of various difficulties, which will influence the way in which her mother and others see her (e.g. the mother may see the child as moody).

Consequences for the Mother-Child Relationship

In many instances, the offender will go even further in his attempts to shift responsibility for his behaviour, and seek to implicate the mother. For example, he may say things like: 'If your mother was more interested in me, I wouldn't have to do this to you.'
Your damn mother and her Victorian morals, there's no place for them here. I'm not going to let you turn out cold like your mother. (Bass & Thornton 1983, p.76)
An effect of this is that the child may become angry with the mother and blame her for the offender's actions and her suffering. He may also undermine the child's belief in the mother's capacity to help, by saying things such as: 'Your mother will have a breakdown if you tell.'

This shifting of responsibility by the offender creates a situation in which the victim is encouraged to feel responsible for protecting the mother from learning the truth. In seeking to shift responsibility and cut the child off from a source of support, thus ensuring secrecy, the offender has given the child intensive coaching in the habit of protecting the mother from upsetting things. This habit frequently remains influential after disclosure, with the child finding it very difficult to be open with her mother.

As the mother is the adult to whom the child is most likely to turn for help, the offender will often try to create a climate of mistrust and division between the victim/s and their mother, commonly telling the child things such as: 'Your mother won't believe you if you tell.' 'Your mother knows what I'm doing and she doesn't care.'

These tactics are likely to have a devastating effect on the mother-child relationship, which may be further distanced or conflictual after disclosure. If they have a history of difficulties as a mother and child prior to the sexual assault, with the mother seeing the child as 'disturbed' or 'naughty' as a result of her experience in trying to manage the child, the offender will often have actively encouraged the mother in these beliefs.

Consequences for the Mother

Following disclosure, the mother's guilt and confusion about what the child says will be exacerbated by virtue of her position as a wife and mother in a society which has strong prescriptions about these roles. For example, she may see herself as inadequate or blame herself for her failure to be a good enough mother to protect her child. This view is based on the ideology of motherhood (Wearing 1984), an influential set of ideas in society prescribing certain standards against which mothers are judged (and judge themselves) according to their adequacy in meeting the standards. This self-blame may have been encouraged by the offender, family members and possibly by other professionals who may have become involved in the situation.

She may be very fearful that fully supporting the child will lead to her losing both her future security and her relationship with the offender. She will experience a dilemma of loyalty about whom to support and may feel overwhelmed by confusion about what action to take. Therefore she will be extremely vulnerable to the tactics of the offender as he attempts to maintain the shield of secrecy. At this time the offender may be denying the assault and be intervening in ways which lead the mother to disbelieve the child, or if she believes her, to think that the child encouraged the sexual contact with him. For example, in order to try to shift responsibility for his behaviour onto the child and confuse the mother, he may be saying things like: 'She led me on, what could I do?' 'She wouldn't leave me alone.' 'Why did she stay up late watching TV with me if she didn't like it?'

He may have laid the groundwork for problems prior to disclosure by lying to the mother about the child. For example, whenever Sally, aged 8 years, threatened to tell her mother what he was doing, Ron would tell her mother that she had been disobedient in order to set the stage where disclosure would appear to be a malicious attempt to avoid punishment for rude and disobedient behaviour towards her father.

This may all result in the mother becoming angry and reactive to the child and blaming her for the sexual assault. The mother will be unaware of the ways that the child has been coached by the offender to keep secret what occurred.

The offender's ploys to ensure that his behaviour remains secret thus create division and mistrust between his victim/s and their mother. It is also likely that the offender's actions will have isolated the child from possible support from siblings. Society for thousands of years has aided and abetted him in this, in that it fosters ignorance about both the existence of incest and the practices of offenders in keeping it secret (Rush 1980).

Because of secrecy around the lies he tells, both the mother and child will be unaware of the extent of the offenders's contributions to their own experiences and reactions, and to the difficulties in their relationship. While the offender's role is largely invisible, the mother and child will often be experiencing damaging guilt and blame in their interactions with one another.

IDEAS ABOUT THERAPY
WHICH OBSCURE THE OFFENDER'S ROLE

The family therapy literature about incest highlights notions of family dysfunction and inadequacy, and, as has been stated earlier, renders invisible the role of the offender. What is brought into focus is the issue of responsibility of both parents, with the mother tending to be more strongly blamed for not correctly fulfilling her role.

Such ways of thinking lead to a therapeutic practice in which, since mothers are seen as culpable or inadequate, the task of the therapist is to assist them to become more competent as parents. The emphasis of such approaches is largely on diagnosis, with the therapist identifying the areas of inadequacy which need to be rectified in relation to the mother's parenting of the child. For example:

Mothers frequently have not bonded with their children and have difficulty empathising with them. (MacFarlane & Waterman 1986, p.232)

The mothers were usually largely responsible for the poor communication since they themselves often served as uncommunicative role models in their interactions with husbands that were observed by the children. (Sgroi 1982, p.194)

Therapy may focus on the mother's inadequacy and how this contributed to the situation of sexual assault and to the difficulties which the child is experiencing:

The therapist's goal is to be a role model to the mother, to educate her, and to gradually shift the focus back to the primary relationship between mother and child. (MacFarlane & Waterman 1986, p.232)

... the women must acknowledge their own failure to prevent the incestuous behaviour by contributing to and permitting the blurring of role boundaries among family members. (Sgroi 1982, p.199)

Therapy for the child will also take a diagnostic direction, with the therapist identifying areas of deficit or damage, offering the child the opportunity to express her feelings, and in various ways providing a venue for healing in the context of individual therapy. For example:

A comprehensive diagnostic assessment should be done in the first three months of individual therapy. (Sgroi 1982, p.142)

The sexually abused child needs to regress and complete her developmental tasks. (Macfarlane & Waterman 1986, p.236)

The diagnostic approach may also be applied to the mother-child relationship, involving things like assessing the interactions of children and mothers according to criteria for functional relationships and teaching mothers other more helpful ways to parent.

It is the interaction between mother and child that is functional or dysfunctional and treatment should work toward improving that interaction. (MacFarlane & Waterman 1986, p.231)

Both mother and daughter need to be aware of role reversal and how and why it needs to be corrected. (Sgroi 1982, p.144)

The outcome of this kind of thinking is a therapy where mothers and children may be seen individually, and in which the responsibility and contributions of the offender may be obscured. This process will not establish a context for the impact of secrecy to be overturned, because it does not offer the mother and child the opportunity to de-brief about their actual experience together and in so doing to 'notice' the impact of the offender's actions on their lives and relationships. The consequence of this is that the cycles of guilt and blame may not be interrupted and the process of healing may be held back. The offender's shield of invisibility stays in place.

THERAPY: UNDERMINING THE IMPACT OF SECRECY

An approach which acknowledges the offender's role

An appreciation of the offender's power in shaping the perceptions of his victim and the mother, casts a different light on our response to the mothers and children who present for therapy following disclosure. For example, a mother may present and believe that her daughter must have initiated the sexual contact in some way, and this belief may be promoting anger and distance between them. Through the lens of the 'dysfunctional family' approach, this would be seen as evidence of the mother's complicity and guilt: having withdrawn as her husband's sexual partner, she has at some level wanted her daughter to take on this role, and in order to cope with her guilt, blames the child. This fails to acknowledge the offender's power ploys over the child, and perpetuates guilt and blame.

An alternative idea, which takes into account the offender's powerful role, is that the relationship problems between mother and child victim which are so commonly seen after incest is disclosed, are more likely to be the result of a campaign of 'disinformation' orchestrated by the offender, under the cover provided by the secrecy which he imposes on the victim. The offender's actions create a context in which the mother and child are blind to his role in creating the difficulties in their relationship and to the resources each of them has to overcome the effects of the sexual assault. The 'fit' between the offender's shifting of responsibility for the sexual assault onto the victim and mother, and notions about gender and responsibility for sexual assault which have broad currency in society, further blind mother and daughter to alternative ways of looking at the situation.

A therapy process which does justice to the concerns of family members must address the specific difficulties being presented by the family members, such as the ones described above. However, we believe that an approach to therapy with these families must also include some opportunity for them to acknowledge the impact on their lives of the offender's actions in some way, and in so doing to acknowledge the specific ways in which he has contributed to the difficulties they experience. Because it is secrecy which has created the conditions for problematic habits and patterns of relating to survive, a crucial goal of therapy is to allow family members to reflect together on the processes whereby secrecy has been promoted and enforced and on its devastating effects on their lives and relationships.

For some time we have been interested in the ideas of Michael White and David Epston, and we consider that the frameworks for therapy which they have been developing offer some useful options for working with mothers and children, including allowing them the opportunity to 'discover' the impact of secrecy on their lives and relationships. Central to the approach we favour is the notion that:

... persons organize and give meaning to their experience through the storying of experience, and (that) in the performance of these stories they express selected aspects of their lived experience ... it is these stories that are constitutive - shaping lives and relationships. (White & Epston 1989, p.20)

White prefers a 'text analogy' for therapy, and this idea has profound implications for working therapeutically with mothers and children where a child has been sexually assaulted. Families presenting for help to therapists can be seen as involved in a dominant or problem-saturated story about themselves and their relationships, with other significant people usually participating in the shaping of the story. The stories presented by families focus largely on people's inadequacy, and aspects of their lived experience which focus on their competence are left out. Alternative stories are not available to families experiencing difficulties as they have not had opportunities to access these stories. In the situation where a child has been sexually assaulted, secrecy has operated to obscure family members' experience of events and to shape their perceptions of each other in various ways, as described earlier. The effect of this is that the dominant story in which the family is involved has been largely authored by the offender rather than by the mother and children themselves. For example, the family may present a picture of the child as being 'naughty' and the mother being unable to control him, and this may be the story which the offender has actively promoted in his tactics to maintain secrecy. Dominant societal stories about mothers' responsibility for everything that happens in families

(Wearing 1984), and about women's responsibility in relationships with men, operate to solidify and give credence to the dominant story.

Therapy based on these notions requires the therapist to assist the family members to locate alternative stories about their experience and to situate themselves in stories which include the whole context of their experience. In the case of child sexual assault, this would include an exploration of the context of each person's experience of their relationship with the offender, thus editing back into the story acknowledgement of how he attempted to author it. This process assists family members to locate responsibility back to the offender, thus undermining the impact of guilt and blame in their lives. Family members will have some opportunity to undermine the impact of societal stories which are oppressive to women and children when they identify the offender's misuse of power in shaping events. This is extremely empowering for family members, because as the process of therapy unfolds, new solutions become available to them in dealing with the difficulties they are facing. Secrecy is thus undermined and the family members take back authorship of their own lives. The shield of invisibility of the offender is lifted. When families begin to ascribe new meanings to their situation and rewrite their story, change and healing become possible.

THE THERAPY PROCESS

Engagement with both Mother and Child

The therapist may be confronted with numerous possibilities which present dilemmas for her about how to manage the therapy: e.g. the child may not have disclosed to the mother but to someone else; or the child and mother may not be speaking to one another or be conflictual; or the mother may feel excluded from previous interventions. It is crucial for the therapist to inform herself about what has already occurred with statutory agencies, and to form some hypothesis about potential engagement issues. If, for example, the intensity of conflict is high, this needs to be understood in the context of all the interventions that have taken place, including the offender's interventions in enforcing secrecy, and not simply in terms of the mother-child relationship. It may be necessary to take some time to clarify this.

The joining process is critical and will determine the extent to which the therapist may closely understand each person's experience, a necessary prerequisite for therapy to take place. This seems especially important in the situation where family members have experienced a variety of different kinds of interviews prior to being referred for therapy, as is usually the case. Where mother and child have had separate interviews, as often occurs, it is useful to spend some time exploring what each has experienced in these separate sessions, how much of this information has been shared, and their feelings about coming together for the therapy session. It is important that the therapist spells out clearly what she knows, who she has spoken to, and who she will be speaking to subsequently.

We believe that, unless the mother and child have a chance early in the process to debrief together on the effect on their relationship of the sexual assault and events subsequent to disclosure, any tension and conflict between them may intensify and this may slow down the healing process for them both.

The overall goal of sessions is to open space for the mother and child to make important discoveries about one another, particularly about their resources. Such discoveries may be rendered impossible if they are being seen separately by different workers, despite the workers' intentions and effectiveness.

An unfortunate side-effect of deciding to deal separately with a mother and child is that secrecy and protection between them may be inadvertently reinforced. This can lead to the mother being less able to see her own (or her child's) resources, and may even inadvertently reinforce her feelings of guilt or anger, particularly where she does not have clear information about her child's progress in therapy. Separate sessions may have the same effect on the child, preventing her from seeing her mother's capacity to nurture her and possibly reinforcing her anger or protectiveness toward her mother.

In arguing for joint mother-child sessions, we recognise that there are situations in which some women are unable to believe their child's disclosure (for many of the reasons already discussed), and that in these situations joint interviews would be unhelpful. Our recommendation for joint sessions does not preclude the offering of additional avenues (individual or group) where women can discuss issues which are inappropriate for mother-child sessions. For example, the child's disclosure may lead to a woman remembering experiences of childhood assault which she may wish to discuss; and many women request an opportunity to discuss their dilemmas about their marriage and the experience of divided loyalty. Children may also benefit from participation in groups of peers who have had similar experiences.

Externalizing the Problem and Exploring the Problem's Influence in the Lives and Relationships of Family Members

The therapist, after engaging with all family members who attend the session, begins by seeking to understand from each person the concerns which are most pressing for them. (The sessions may be attended by siblings who were not assaulted, in addition to the mother and victim/s). In many situations, there will be a range of concerns presented, and the family may be asked to rank them in order. In seeking to understand each person's experience of the presented difficulties, the therapist uses language in particular ways. 'Externalizing the problem' is a key aspect of the therapeutic approach developed by Michael White, who points out (1988/89) that the way in which the therapist talks about the problem, contributes to the construction of the problem.

'Externalizing' is an approach to therapy that encourages persons to objectify, and at times, to personify, the problems that they experience as oppressive. In this process, the problem becomes a separate entity and thus external to the person who was, or the relationship that was, ascribed the problem. Those problems that are considered to be inherent, and those relatively fixed qualities that are attributed to persons and relationships, are rendered less fixed and less restricting. (p.3)

In talking with mothers and children about the problems which concern them, the therapist seeks to use language which reflects their experience of the problem, and which locates the problem outside the persons or their relationship.

For example, it is common for children who have suffered sexual assault and the upheaval of disclosure and subsequent intervention, to report that their lives are crippled and restricted by fears and anxiety. By externalizing fear, the therapist is able to explore the effects of fear on all aspects of the child's life and relationships. One effect of talking in this way is to imply that the fear has not totally overtaken the child.

In exploring the effect of fear on the child's life, it is useful to ask the child and family about their understanding of how fear was able to become so influential in their lives. This may provoke the child or other family members to 'notice' the role of the offender in encouraging and promoting fear's hold on the child. If the child and family are mystified about how fear got such a hold, the therapist may ask if there were any things which the offender did or said which may have contributed to the growth of fear in the family. As the child describes the things which the offender has said or done, the mother and other family members may hear for the first time the particular types of threats and intimidations to which the child has been subjected on an ongoing basis. The opportunity arises for the child's difficulties to begin to be seen in a new way - that is, in the context of the offender's behaviour, rather than as other examples of the child's individual 'disturbance'.

For example: one child described how the offender would often come into her room and just stand there for what seemed like hours. She would lie there in terror, not knowing whether or not this would be one of the times when he would assault her.

Another told how he had been convinced that he would be put into a home and never see his mother and young brother again if anyone ever found out about the sexual assault.

Frequently, mothers and children who come for the therapy describe various problems which they have experienced in being able to talk about the sexual assault and the impact on their lives of disclosure and subsequent intervention. Mothers often feel excluded and unable to find ways in which to talk to their children - it may seem that police and counsellors know more than they do about their child's feelings and reactions. They may blame themselves for not having seen what was going on, and may torture themselves with guilt. They may be mystified as to why the child did not tell them about the sexual assault, and may wonder if this means that the child in some way initiated or enjoyed the sexual contact. The child may feel that their mother does not understand what they have been through, and may be angry with their mother for reasons which have been discussed earlier.

A helpful way to talk about these difficulties in the mother-child relationship is to externalize secrecy. Frequently, in offering mothers and children the opportunity to 'debrief' together about the impact of disclosure and its sequelae, an exploration about the effects of secrecy on their lives and relationships provides a way in which they can begin to talk together in a different way, without falling into old patterns of guilt and blame. This may be in marked contrast to their previous attempts to talk, which may have provoked angry outbursts and promoted further cycles of distance and resentment. They may be asked for example:

- *How has secrecy affected the way in which your relationship has developed over the past few years?*
- *What has secrecy prevented you from finding out from your daughter that it would have been important for you to know?*

Questions such as these enable the therapists and family to explore the effects of the problem (secrecy) on their lives and relationships. Exploring the problem in this way reduces guilt and blame, as the mother and children are invited to discover together the impact of secrecy on each of them and on their relationship.

When well engaged with the family, the therapist can introduce other questions which can enable mothers and children to discover together the offender's role in their difficulties. For example, the child/ren may be asked:

- *Were there any ways in which ..... (the offender) coached/encouraged secrecy?*
- *How was he able to convince you that your mother wouldn't be on your side?*

When children who have been sexually assaulted answer questions such as these, the mother may hear for the first time, how the offender was able to entrap the child in a web of silence. This new information can be highly influential in the mother beginning to see the child in a new way, because the offender's responsibility for the assault becomes clearer, and his manipulation of the child's powerless position is exposed.

Where the offender has deceived and tricked the mother, it is sometimes very powerful to externalize trickery. The mother may be asked:

- *In what ways was ..... able to blind you with trickery about what he was doing?*
- *What is your understanding of the ways ..... was able to pull the wool over your eyes about what was going on?*

When children hear their mother talk in response to questions such as these, they have the opportunity to see her and her behaviour in a different way, and may themselves initiate further questions about the offender's actions and tricks.

Asking questions such as these creates a context in which the mother and child are invited to discover together the offender's role in dividing and deceiving them. As further questions are introduced, they may become aware of the capacity of their relationship to avoid being totally overwhelmed by these manoeuvres.

Exploring the Influence of Family Members in the Life of the Problem

After thoroughly exploring with the family the effects of the problem on their lives and on the mother-child relationship, the therapist begins to ask different types of questions, questions which seek to find out about the occasions when the mother and child and their relationship managed to avoid being overwhelmed or defeated by the problem. These are termed 'unique outcome' questions (White 1988). For example, the therapist may ask the child:

- *Given your father's encouragement of secrecy, were there any times when you were able to stand up to secrecy and tell someone about the abuse that was happening to you?*

Both may be asked:

- *Have there been any times since this came out into the open, that you two have been able to overcome secrecy and talk about what you have both been through?*

To the mother:

- *Have there been any times when guilt could have held you back from thinking that there was any way you could help your daughter, but you overcame it and reached out to her?*

Questions such as these require that family members select out examples of their competence in the face of problems. For example, in asking about the times when secrecy has not totally dominated people's lives, the therapist and family may find out about the ways in which courage has been practised in the face of great intimidation; or in asking about victories over fear, accounts of someone being brave, or persistent in the face of fear, may unfold.

**Further Questions Which Assist in the 'Re-authoring'
of the Mother-Child Relationship**

Once a unique outcome is identified, the therapist introduces other types of questions which invite a 'performance of meaning'; in answering these questions together, and hearing the response of each other to these questions, a new story of their relationship is constructed. For example the mother may be asked:

- *Despite the hold that secrecy had over your family, how do you think your daughter was able to tell someone about what her father was doing?*
- *What does it tell you about your daughter that she was able to stand up to secrecy with such courage?*
- *Given the way in which ..... (offender) enforced a secrecy lifestyle in the family, how is it that you were able to tell people outside the family about such upsetting things, in order to get help for your sons?*

The child or young person may be asked questions such as:

- *Despite the strong hold which secrecy had on you, how were you able to stand up to it and tell someone what was happening?*
- *What does it tell you about your future, knowing that you have been faced with a situation of great fear and intimidation, and that you took strong action to escape it?*

As the mother hears her son or daughter answer questions such as these, she will often become aware for the first time of the resourcefulness of the young person. Such information about her child may begin to dispel fears about 'damage' or 'disturbance' which may have been unhelpful, and may have prevented her from being able to understand her child's experience of oppression and abuse. Similarly, the child is able to hear her mother acknowledging her resourcefulness, and is able to see the way in which her mother has also withstood secrecy in order to listen to the child's disclosure. Both may be asked:

- *What do you think that I am learning about your relationship as I hear about how you two were able to avoid your relationship being totally overwhelmed by the effects of secrecy?*

Both mother and child are involved in re-authoring the story of their relationship, a new story in which the offender's role is visible, and in which their relationship's resilience in the face of secrecy is acknowledged. They are invited through the questions to experience themselves and their relationship differently as the new story unfolds.

CASE EXAMPLE

The following case example highlights some of the points discussed:

The E. family, comprising Marie (mother), Donna (10) and Brian (8), were seen for therapy some months following the children's disclosure that their father had sexually assaulted them. The offender was no longer living with the family. In the initial sessions, there had been discussion of the ways in which the children had developed a habit of protecting their mother from hearing anything which might upset her or worry her. They had been coached in this by their father who had consistently undermined their mother's competence in the family by belittling her with constant criticism. They also felt guilty for the stress which their mother had suffered in dealing with the welfare and legal system following their disclosure.

As we were discussing some ways in which Donna and Brian had recently begun to overcome their habit of protecting their mother by keeping worrying things to themselves, Donna started to cry and said that she was 'frightened all the time'. While she wanted to join in activities with her friends, she could not, since she was afraid to leave her home unless her mother went with her.

In this instance, fear was externalized and its effects on Donna's life explored. It appeared that fear was severely restricting her activities and stopping her from doing things which she would have enjoyed. Marie was shocked to hear about the extent of the crippling effects of fear on her daughter's life. While she had worried that Donna seemed 'nervous' and had spent a lot of time at home, she had no appreciation of the extent to which Donna was being oppressed by fear. She invited Donna to move and sit with her as we explored the effect of fear on Donna and on her mother and brother. Her mother told Donna that she was very sad to think that fear had got in the way of Donna asking for help from her. Brian began to talk about his difficulties in getting to sleep at night, and fear seemed to be the culprit here also.

When the therapist asked Donna and Brian how they thought that fear had taken such a hold on them Donna cried and said that their father had told them that if they ever told about the sexual assaults, he would kill their baby brother. Marie was visibly shocked on hearing this, and said that this was the first time that she had heard about this threat. She proceeded to reassure the children about the plans which she had made to ensure the family's safety.

The therapist noted that this discussion during the session seemed to be quite a departure from both children's habit of protecting their mother from hearing upsetting things, and from being silenced by fear (unique outcomes). The therapist then invited Marie, Donna and Brian to speculate on how they thought that Donna and Brian had been able to stand up so forcefully to old habits and to fear; on what that told their mother about their courage and resourcefulness; and on what the children had learnt about their mother's ability to assist them.

In the following session, the family reported that fear was becoming increasingly less influential in Donna's and Brian's lives.

CONCLUSION

Talking with mothers and children in the ways discussed in this chapter, can open space for them to make important discoveries about themselves and their relationship, discoveries which open possibilities for them to see their relationship in new ways, and thus to develop new ways of dealing with their lives in the aftermath of sexual assault.

ACKNOWLEDGEMENTS

We would like to thank our colleagues Catherine Munro and Chris Burke for their time in reading the drafts of this chapter and for their insightful and helpful comments and suggestions. We also thank the families with whom we have worked from whom we have learnt through the sharing of their experiences. We would also like to acknowledge the participants in the training workshops which we have conducted over the past three years.

REFERENCES

Bass, E. & Thornton, L. (Eds.) 1983:
'**I Never Told Anyone.' Writings by Women Survivors of Child Sexual Abuse**.
Harper & Row, New York.

Brickman, J. 1984:
'Feminist, nonsexist, and traditional models of therapy: implications for working
with incest.'**Women & Therapy**, 3:49-67.

Conte, J.R. 1985:
'Clinical dimensions of adult sexual abuse of children.' **Behavioural Sciences &
the Law**, 3:341-354.

Dietz, C.A. & Craft, J.L. 1980:
'Family dynamics of incest: a new perspective.' **Social Casework**, 61:602-609.

Eist, H.I. & Mandel, A.U. 1968:
'Family treatment of ongoing incest behaviour.'**Family Process**, 7:216-232.

Finkelhor, D. 1984:
Child Sexual Abuse: New theory and research. The Free Press, New York.

Finkelhor, D. 1986:
A Sourcebook on Child Sexual Abuse. Sage Publications, Beverley Hills.

Giaretto, H. 1982:
Integrated treatment of child sexual abuse. Science & Behaviour Books Inc., Palo
Alto.

Goldman, R.J. & Goldman, J.D.G. 1988:
'The prevalence and nature of child sexual abuse in Australia.'**Australian Journal
of Sex, Marriage & Family**, 9:94-106.

Gutheil, T.G. & Avery, N.C. 1977:
'Multiple overt incest as family defence against loss.' **Family Process**, 16:105-
116.

Herman, J.L. 1981:
Father-Daughter Incest. Harvard University Press, Cambridge, Massachusetts.

Horowitz, A.N. 1983:
'Guidelines for treating father-daughter incest.'**Social Casework**, 69:515-524.

Jenkins, A. 1988:
'Engaging the male incest perpetrator.' Workshop Notes.

Kowalski, K. 1988:
'The importance of mothers in the treatment of sexually abused adolescent females.'
Dulwich Centre Newsletter, Summer.

Laing, L. & Kamsler, A. 1989:
Sexual Assault Counselling Workshops for Health Workers.

Lustig, Capt.N., Dresser, Capt.J.W., Spellman, Maj.S.W. & Murray, Maj.T.B. 1966:
'Incest: a family group survival pattern.'**Archives of General Psychiatry**, 14:31-40.

MacFarlane, K. & Waterman, J. 1986:
Sexual abuse of young children. The Guildford Press, New York.

Machotka, P., Pittman, F.S. & Flomenhaft, K. 1967:
'Incest as a family affair.'**Family Process**, 6:98-116.

McIntyre, K. 1981:
'Role of mothers and father-daughter incest: a feminist analysis.' **Social Work**,
26:462-466.

Rush, F. 1980:
The Best Kept Secret: Sexual abuse of children. Prentice-Hall. Englewood Cliffs,
New Jersey.

Russell, D.E.H. 1986:
The Secret Trauma. Basic Books, New York.

Sgroi, S.M. 1982:
Handbook of Clinical Intervention in Child Abuse. Lexington Books, Massachusetts.

Summit, R. 1983:
'The child abuse accommodation syndrome.'**Child Abuse & Neglect**, 7:177-193.

Waldby, C. 1985:
'Breaking the Silence.' A report based upon the findings of the **Women Against Incest Phone-In Survey**. Honeysett Printing Group.

Ward, E. 1984:
Father Daughter Rape. The Women's Press Ltd., London.

Wattenberg, E. 1985:
'In a different light: a feminist perspective on the role of mothers in father-daughter incest.'**Child Welfare**, 64:203-211.

Wearing, B. 1984:
The Ideology of Motherhood. Allen & Unwin, Sydney.

White, M. 1988:
'The process of questioning: a therapy of literary merit?' **Dulwich Centre Newsletter**, Winter.

White, M. 1988/89:
'The externalizing of the problem.'**Dulwich Centre Newsletter**, Summer.

White, M. & Epston, D. 1989:
Literate Means to Therapeutic Ends. Dulwich Centre Publications, Adelaide.

CONTRIBUTING AUTHORS & EDITORS

Janet Adams-Westcott:

Janet is a psychologist who is the Director of the Family Sexual Abuse Treatment Program of Family & Children's Service in Tulsa, Oklahoma. She applies second order cybernetic family therapy approaches in her work with victims of child sexual abuse and their families. Janet teaches at local universities and conducts professional workshops on family therapy and family violence.

Michael Durrant:

Michael is a psychologist who is the Director of Eastwood Family Therapy Centre in Sydney, New South Wales. He has co-ordinated a children-at-risk team and provided services to children and families where abuse has occurred. He teaches family therapy widely in Australia, New Zealand and North America.

Richard Elms:

Richard is a social worker who is a therapist with the Wentworth Area Health Services, in New South Wales. Richard supervises other therapists and consults to staff of other agencies who work with adolescents who have experienced violence and abuse. He also has considerable experience in working with sexual abuse offenders in residential care contexts.

Irene Esler:

Irene is a social worker who is Director of Leslie Centre in Auckland, New Zealand. She has worked in the area of community mental health for the past twelve years and, in her work, has a strong focus on the political and social contexts of the problems that persons bring to therapy. This includes attention to the context of patriarchy.

Deanna Isenbart:

Deanna is a psychologist who is a therapist at Family & Children's Service in Tulsa, Oklahoma. She has been working with victims of sexual abuse and their families for seven years. Deanna's initial interest in rituals developed as a result of her girlhood in rural western Oklahoma, where she participated with family and friends in developing rituals which enhanced a sense of community and eased the experience of growing into adulthood.

Amanda Kamsler:

Amanda is a psychologist who is a family therapist, supervisor and teacher in private practice in Sydney, New South Wales. She is also a consultant to various teams in the community, including to Dympna House, which provides services to women who have been abused.

Kate Kowalski:

Kate is a family therapist in practice at the Eastwood Family Therapy Centre in Sydney, New South Wales. She is a former faculty member of the Brief Family Therapy Centre of Milwaukee, and has taught widely in Australia and North America. Sexual abuse has been a major focus of her work.

Lesley Laing:

Lesley is a social worker and family therapist who is co-ordinator of the New South Wales Sexual Assault Education Unit. She has been working in the field of child sexual assault for the past six years, and is interested in developing theoretical approaches which reflect a feminist analysis of sexual assault. She is presently involved in developing resources and training courses to assist health workers in their work with victims of sexual assault.

Jane Waldegrave:

Jane is a therapist in private practice in Auckland who has considerable experience in working with victims of sexual abuse. She is interested in addressing the political, social and cultural context of abuse, and works to assist persons to challenge the constraints of gender issues.

Cheryl White:

Cheryl has a background in social work and has worked in a broad range of clinical areas. She is currently the Editor of Dulwich Centre Publications, Adelaide.